IRELAND 1970-2020

Colum Kenny

Gretton Books
Cambridge

Colum Kenny

First published in 2024 by Gretton Books

© Colum Kenny 2024

The moral right of Colum Kenny to be identified as the author of this work has been asserted in accordance with the Copyright, Design and Patents Act 1988

All rights reserved. Apart from any use permitted under UK copyright law no part of this publication may be reproduced, stored in a retrieval system, or transmitted, in any form or by any means without the prior written permission of the publisher, nor be otherwise circulated in any form of binding or cover other than that in which it is published and without a similar condition being imposed on the subsequent purchaser.

A CIP catalogue record for this title is available from the British Library.

ISBN 978-1-7392067-5-8

Printed and bound by 4edge in the UK

Ireland 1970-2020

CONTENTS

1	What's in a name?	1
2	Introduction	3
3	Changes: 1970-1979	5
4	Set-Backs: 1980-1989	24
5	Birth of the Celtic Tiger: 1990-1999	37
6	Boom and Bust: 2000-2009	56
7	Recovery: 2010-2020	69
8	Into the Future	86
	Additional reading	90

ILLUSTRATIONS

'Bloody Sunday' 1972	8
Mary Robinson elected President in 1990	39
Mo Mowlam UK Secretary of State for Northern Ireland 1998	52
Gaelic Athletic Association welcomes diversity in sport, 2020	63
Lesbian and Gay Pride Day, Dublin 2003	75

Colum Kenny

To Ireland in the Coming Times

for my granddaughters Aoife and Sophie

– born 2022 –

What's in a name?

Ireland is an island in the Atlantic inhabited by seven million people. It is today divided by a border. Its close neighbour Britain long occupied the whole island and colonised some of it.

The Republic of Ireland (population 5.1 million, formerly **the Irish Free State** from 1922 until 1949) and **Northern Ireland** (population 1.9 million) are the two parts of Ireland. The border between them was drawn when the United Kingdom partitioned Ireland in 1920.

The Republic is a short form of 'the Republic of Ireland', a member of the European Union. Use of the name 'Ireland' to mean the Republic alone is misleading. Irish citizens prefer 'Republic of Ireland' over 'Irish republic', which can seem diminishing. Most republicans in Ireland today do not support IRA or other unlawful violent paramilitaries.

The United Kingdom is a state consisting of Great Britain and Northern Ireland. From 1800 until 1922 the UK included all of the island of Ireland.

Great Britain includes England, Scotland and Wales but not Ireland or even Northern Ireland.

'**British**' is a form of identity shared by a minority of Irish people. Many of that minority are descended from British settlers and live in Northern Ireland.

The British Isles is a geographic designation used by some British people to include Ireland, but thus used is not regarded as accurate by most Irish people. The Irish Celts and British Celts were separate branches of the Celts, and Ireland has never been a part of Great Britain constitutionally.

Éire is a name of the island of Ireland in the old language (Gaelic/Irish). Most Irish people now speak English as their first language, although most schools also teach Irish. The official name of the independent state (the Republic) is 'Éire' or 'Ireland'. This was a 1937 constitutional assertion that reflected a rejection in principle of Northern Ireland and of the partition of Ireland. In practice (and explicitly under the Belfast/Good Friday Agreement) the Republic of Ireland has always accepted that Irish unity must be achieved only by mutual consent.

Southern Ireland is a misleading term for the Republic, with the most northern point of the island being within the Republic in Co. Donegal. Citizens of the Republic seldom use the term, although they often use 'the north' and 'the south' as informal designations.

Ulster, one of four old provinces of Ireland, consists of nine of the 32 Irish counties. Northern Ireland, which was created by the British in 1920 – in a manner intended to ensure that Northern Ireland's electorate would have a solid pro-British unionist majority – consists of just the six counties of north-eastern Ulster. Thus, it is wrong to equate Northern Ireland with Ulster.

Dáil Éireann and a senate (***'Seanad Éireann'***) constitute the Republic's parliament in Dublin. The ***taoiseach*** is the Republic's prime minister, the ***tánaiste*** his or her deputy. The **Northern Ireland Assembly**, a devolved government of the UK, sits at **Stormont** in Belfast. Northern Irish voters also elect MPs to the UK parliament at **Westminster**.

Introduction

Ireland is known internationally for its resistance to British rule, for its Catholic missionaries, and for many writers such as James Joyce and Samuel Beckett who have grappled with what was a conservative and conventionally religious society. But the island has changed much in recent decades.

The United Kingdom partitioned Ireland in 1920, unwilling to surrender part of Ulster despite a republican landslide in most of Ireland in the UK general election of 1918. The independent Irish state that was created in 1921–22 has lately grown confident, liberal and relatively wealthy. Yet inequalities remain. An arrogance that arose from rapid economic growth exacerbated the financial crisis of 2008 and this has left a legacy of problems. There is a shortage of affordable accommodation – some say a housing crisis. The Irish state is also unduly dependent on foreign direct investment that is encouraged by generous tax incentives. Meanwhile, in Northern Ireland discrimination against Catholics has been confronted, but a pro-British core of committed unionists seems averse to radical new initiatives and peace is fragile.

Irish people, overall, have embraced membership of the European Union. Northern Ireland's recent departure from the European Union, as an integral part of the United Kingdom, was against the wishes of a majority of the people of Northern Ireland. The Republic's government regards Brexit as a threat to the Belfast/Good Friday Agreement of 1998 that helped to bring peace in Northern Ireland, after years of civil strife and violence between nationalists and unionists. Peace ensured that the EU single market could work as intended, without disruption by intrusive security checks at the Irish border. Brexit now divides the EU from the UK on Irish soil. It has raised the possibility of there being once more a hard border on the island of Ireland, which few Irish people regard as desirable and which most business representatives both north and south of the border oppose. A special Northern Ireland Protocol agreed by the British and the EU as part of Brexit addressed this issue, but unionists denounced its terms as threatening to the union of Northern Ireland with Britain.

During the present century the Republic of Ireland became the first country to legalise same-sex marriage by referendum, with almost two out of every three voters approving of it. For much of the twentieth century the Irish state banned abortion and the sale of contraceptives and exercised a rigid censorship of books and films, but this has changed.

While change in the Republic of Ireland partly reflects growing economic prosperity, a prosperity that is evident too in the unprecedented arrival of skilled and unskilled migrants needed to fill jobs, the province of Northern Ireland has stagnated and is heavily dependent on state investment from Britain. Where business in Belfast had outshone that in Dublin in the early twentieth century, the position was reversed by the dawn of the twenty-first. Developments during the past fifty years have made practicable the possibility of a new and productive relationship between the two separate parts of the island of Ireland.

Changes: 1970-1979

If there was an historic tipping-point in Ireland during the twentieth century, a time when major changes north and south of the Irish border became inevitable, it was during the early months of 1972.

In Northern Ireland, on 30 January 1972, British paratroopers opened fire on a civil rights demonstration in the city of Derry (also known as Londonderry), killing fourteen marchers. In the Republic of Ireland, on 10 May 1972, an overwhelming majority of the electorate voted in a referendum for their state to join the European Economic Community (from 1993 the 'European Union' or 'EU'). This decision was made without prejudice to the continuing military neutrality of the independent Irish state, itself just fifty years old then.

The first event, highly visible and violent, marked the failure of a policy that for half a century had seen the government in London leave the UK province of Northern Ireland largely to itself. After Britain partitioned Ireland in 1920, a Protestant majority in Northern Ireland that supported continuing political union with Britain distrusted and oppressed a Catholic minority that was largely nationalist. There was discrimination in employment in the public service, and in the allocation of housing and other social benefits. Constituencies were 'gerrymandered' (fixed) by the unionist majority to disadvantage nationalist voters.

The second major event of 1972, which was celebrated throughout the Republic, reflected a new level of economic and political confidence in the independent Irish state. For decades after the state's creation in 1922, its population had fitfully declined, continuing a trend that stemmed partly from the disastrous great famine of the 1840s when starvation and emigration blighted the land. So many departed for the

USA that people who remained along the rugged west coast of Ireland – which today is rebranded for tourists as 'The Wild Atlantic Way' – came to refer wryly to America as 'the next parish'. Poised between Boston and Berlin, the new state later struggled to survive. A powerful and conservative Catholic hierarchy came to dominate its public policy. Joining the European Economic Community (EEC) marked a willingness to go in new directions. Economic protectionism yielded to free trade.

Due to industrial activities such as shipbuilding, as well as other factors, by the first decade of the twentieth century north-eastern Ulster was the most prosperous part of Ireland. However, by the first decade of the twentieth century the Republic had come to eclipse it. In 1911 Belfast was the largest city in Ireland. Today Dublin far surpasses it, with the Republic's capital city having recovered the status it enjoyed before Britain subsumed Ireland fully into the United Kingdom in 1800.

From 1169, when a mixed force of Anglo-Normans and Welsh and other armed men loyal to the English king landed on the south-east coast of Ireland, London had eventually come to control some or all of Ireland. The relationship was further complicated from the sixteenth century, when England adopted Protestantism as its official religion but Ireland remained largely Roman Catholic. After centuries of Irish rebellion and resistance, including a war of independence that followed the great Sinn Féin republican victory in Ireland in the UK general election of 1918, British forces withdrew from most of the island. The new province of Northern Ireland – part of the United Kingdom but with a subsidiary parliament in Belfast – included an oppressed minority of Catholic nationalists. Indeed, two of the six counties of Northern Ireland – Tyrone and Fermanagh – had clear Catholic electoral majorities. Sinn Féin's

Arthur Griffith and Michael Collins believed when they negotiated the agreement for an Anglo-Irish treaty with Britain in 1921 that these and other areas along the new border would be given a chance to opt into the Irish Free State. This was not to be, and the Catholic minority in Northern Ireland felt abandoned.

In February 1967 the Northern Ireland Civil Rights Association (NICRA) was created, inspired by the US civil rights movement and marking a new kind of assertion on the part of those who believed that Northern Ireland badly needed to be reformed. The reaction of authorities was hostile, and there were clashes between activists and police. In October 1968 police baton-charged a peaceful civil rights march in Derry, in full sight of TV cameras and an international audience. Early in 1969 police failed to protect a four-day march from Belfast to Derry, organised by a group named People's Democracy and evoking the spirit of the Selma to Montgomery march in Alabama three years earlier. Violent unionists attacked it at Burntollet Bridge. In August 1969 the government in London felt compelled by the level of disorder to deploy the British Army on the streets of Northern Ireland, where its troops remained for decades.

From the 1970s Northern Ireland became bogged down in a spiral of violence known as 'the Troubles' – a term popularly used too when Ireland was earlier rent asunder by the War of Independence between 1918 and 1921. As it happens J.G. Farrell's uncannily prescient novel *Troubles*, set in the earlier period and part of his empire trilogy, was published in 1970. In 1970 too the Social Democratic and Labour Party (SDLP) was founded in Northern Ireland, in an effort to move voters away from the usual nationalist/unionist polarisation. This party became most closely associated with John Hume, its leader from 1979 to 2001. But extremists on each side regularly outflanked Hume and other moderates. Both in Northern Ireland and the Republic the consequences of the partition of the island in 1920 have continued to shape the contours of political life. This fact, and the fact that the island's economy was heavily agricultural through much of the twentieth century, has meant conservatism was general and socialists struggled to make an impact.

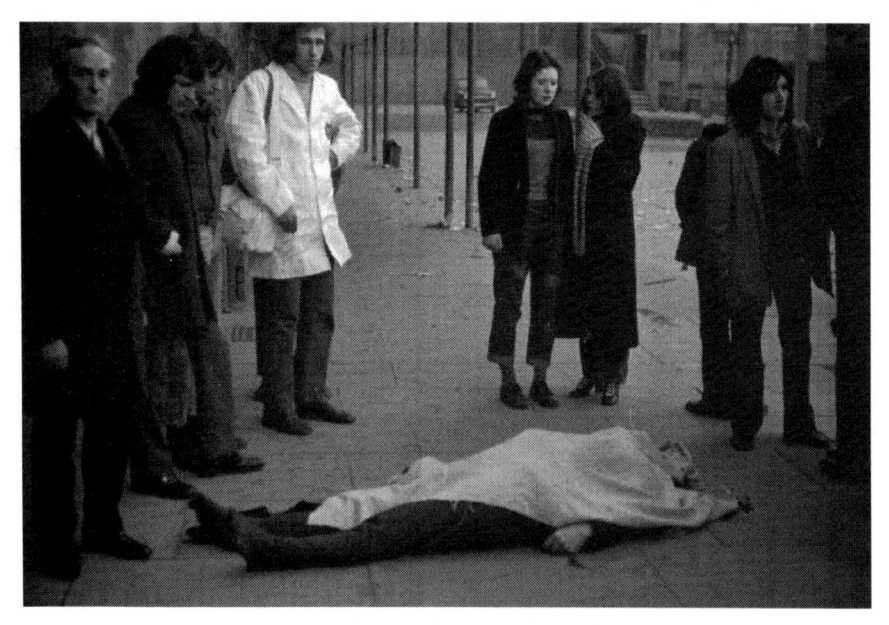

Innocent victims of the Irish 'Troubles' included those (as here) killed by the British Army on 'Bloody Sunday' 1972. Photographer Colman Doyle. *Courtesy National Library of Ireland.*

On the nationalist/Catholic side too has been the Irish Republican Army (IRA), an illegal paramilitary force tracing its lineage back to the armed volunteers who fought Britain on behalf of Sinn Féin in the War of Independence between 1918 and 1921. The old IRA had broad public support that the British tried to ignore. For Sinn Féin, founded by Arthur

Griffith in 1905–06, had been revived following the 1916 Rising in Dublin and swept to victory in Ireland at the UK general election of 1918. Its unity was shattered by the Irish civil war of 1921–22, and the bulk of its political support was absorbed into the two main political parties in the new state, the centre-right Fianna Fáil and Fine Gael (with the new state's army absorbing many volunteers of the old IRA). A rump of Sinn Féin remained, seeing itself as a continuation of the true Sinn Féin. It refused to recognise the new state from 1922 and did not take seats in parliament. This Sinn Féin was itself beset by further splits. In 1969–70, when Sinn Féin became overtly socialist or even Marxist and decided to participate in parliament, some of its members left in protest. Those remaining became known as 'Official Sinn Féin', but by 1982 were 'the Workers' Party'. The breakaway group at first styled itself 'Provisional Sinn Féin' but, from the late 1980s, simply 'Sinn Féin'. The paramilitaries associated with this group, 'the Provisional IRA', became generally known as 'the Provos'. Further splits have seen dissident groups such as 'the Continuity IRA' and 'the Real IRA' emerge.

In the 1970s a substantial number of nationalists saw the Provos as a necessary evil, a means of defending Northern Ireland's Catholics against state or sectarian violence, even as most nationalists disapproved of many IRA actions. Probably for this reason, there was a reluctance among Irish nationalists and in the Irish media generally to use the word 'terrorist' to describe the IRA. On the unionist/Protestant side there were violent paramilitary groups too. 'Loyalists' such as Ian Paisley, a raucous clergyman, drowned out the voices of more moderate unionists and could rely on their own side's paramilitaries to back up their cries of 'no surrender'. On 30 September 1971 Paisley founded the Democratic

Unionist Party. Later, in an unlikely arrangement, a coalition of extremes would come to govern Northern Ireland when Sinn Féin and the Democratic Unionist Party agreed to share power.

As riots and civil unrest continued in Northern Ireland, the British government introduced internment without trial there from 9 August 1971. It was counter-productive, not least because those interned were reported to be all from the Catholic/nationalist side of the conflict and many had no active or significant involvement with paramilitary organisations. During August 1971 loyalist mobs drove thousands of Catholics from their homes. The IRA actively defended Catholic areas against sectarian attacks. It also attacked security forces, with a view to the old nationalist objective of undermining British authority in Ireland.

In 1971, under the cover of internment, the UK government selected some internees for an experiment in interrogation and mistreatment at a specially fitted centre. The internees, none of whom were charged with or convicted of any offence, were subjected to techniques that the British security services had developed elsewhere in their empire and that were similar to some of those later deployed in Iraq by US and other forces. The techniques included white noise, sleep deprivation, hooding, continuous standing against a wall and the withholding of food and water. In 1972 Prime Minister Ted Heath ordered that these techniques not be used. The Republic of Ireland subsequently took the matter to the European Court of Human Rights, which in 1978 held that prisoners had been subjected to inhuman and degrading treatment and that this was a breach of Article 3 of the Convention on Human Rights. Applying case law of the time, the court decided not to describe the treatment as 'torture'. Decades later, in 2014, RTE Television in Dublin published documentary material from UK archives that revealed that in 1977 the UK Home Secretary Merlyn Rees told Prime Minister James Callaghan that UK government ministers had given informed authorisation for the treatment – which Rees then described as 'torture'. In late 2021, as British authorities continued to resist some of the demands of those who had been tortured, the UK Supreme Court found on an application by Margaret McQuillan and others that 'it is likely that the deplorable treatment to which the Hooded Men were subjected at the hands of the security forces would be characterised today, applying the standards of 2021, as torture' ([2021] UKSC 55). It was torture then too.

On Sunday 30 January 1972 about fifteen thousand people gathered in Derry City for a peaceful march to protest against internment without trial. The Northern Ireland government had banned such protests. The British Army was deployed. Local youths and soldiers clashed. The army used rubber bullets, tear gas and water cannons. Members of the Parachute Regiment moved to make arrests in the Bogside area, opening fire on the unarmed crowd with more than one hundred rounds of live ammunition. Extended television coverage on the BBC and elsewhere shocked viewers. Prince Charles (later king) was then commander-in-chief of the Parachute Regiment. 'Bloody Sunday', as the day became known, sealed the fate of Northern Ireland as the place had functioned since 1920.

The first official enquiry into events that day, by the Widgery Tribunal, was widely seen as a whitewash intended to exonerate the authorities. Thirty-eight years after Bloody Sunday, relatives finally received a formal apology from the British government. Speaking in the House of Commons in June 2010, when the report of the Saville inquiry into Bloody Sunday was published, Prime Minister David Cameron admitted that some members of the armed forces had 'acted wrongly ... on behalf of our country, I am deeply sorry.' He added, 'The conclusions of this report are absolutely clear. There is no doubt, there is nothing equivocal, there are no ambiguities. What happened on Bloody Sunday was both unjustified and unjustifiable. It was wrong.' He admitted that Saville had found that 'despite the contrary evidence given by the soldiers' there were that day no attacks or threatened attacks on the army by nail or petrol bombers. Yet relatives of the killed and injured are still seeking justice today.

Within days of Bloody Sunday, the British embassy in Dublin was attacked and set on fire during a protest march. The conflict in Northern Ireland entered a bitter and bloodier phase. Nationalists were determined that never again would Northern Ireland be dominated as it had been by unionists. In March 1972 the UK government recognised that the Northern Ireland parliament at Stormont had failed and abolished it in favour of direct rule from Westminster, which itself was a form of government unacceptable to nationalists. On 21 July 1972 the IRA exploded almost two dozen bombs across the province, killing nine people and seriously wounding scores more. This became known as 'Bloody Friday'.

The UK government held a referendum within Northern Ireland on 8 March 1973, asking if Northern Ireland should remain in the United Kingdom or unite with the Republic. Nationalist leaders condemned the exercise as an inflammatory and sectarian headcount. Nationalist voters were urged to boycott it. Just under 59% of the electorate voted, overwhelmingly in favour of the union with Britain. On the day of the poll, the Provisional IRA exploded several bombs, killing and injuring people –

including outside the Old Bailey Courthouse in London. A Catholic was murdered by Loyalist paramilitaries. Internment without trial in Northern Ireland continued until 1975.

At times during the 1970s the cycle of violence in Northern Ireland seemed to be spinning out of control and incidents were too numerous to be listed here. Secret talks between 'Provo' paramilitaries and British ministers failed to produce a solution. As more British troops poured into Northern Ireland, the catalogue of violence and tit-for-tat attacks showed no prospect of ending. The IRA extended its bombing campaign, including to public houses in England packed with unsuspecting people out for the night. Abuses by security forces and miscarriages of justice exacerbated bad feelings. Six innocent Irishmen, for example, were to spend sixteen years in jail for IRA bombings in Birmingham, although eventually vindicated. Their case was highlighted by Chris Mullin in his book *Error of Judgement*. The 'Guildford Four' were likewise wrongly convicted of crimes committed by 'Provos', their story being later told in the Oscar-nominated 1993 film *In the Name of the Father*. The innocent were framed while those guilty of the bombings stayed free.

*

It would be hard to exaggerate the economic, social and psychological implications of the Republic of Ireland joining the European Economic Community on 1 January 1973. In a referendum in 1972, more than four out of every five voters had backed membership of the EEC. They saw it as likely to help liberate Ireland from its very heavy dependence on British markets and as likely to help liberalise the state's social policies generally. The United Kingdom of Great Britain and Northern Ireland joined the EEC on the same day.

Ireland had significant historical associations with other European countries, especially those such as France and Spain that were Catholic. During the 1960s senior politicians and leading economists in Ireland decided that membership of the EEC was necessary to help the Irish state tackle poverty, high unemployment and emigration – not least by attracting foreign investment. However, it was not then feasible for Ireland to be a member unless the United Kingdom also joined. So, during the 1960s, when France's President Charles de Gaulle made it clear that he did not want Britain within the community, the Republic of Ireland felt obliged to wait. In 1969 De Gaulle's successor Georges Pompidou dropped the veto.

Not only did membership of the EEC open the Republic to new markets for its farm produce, but it also made the state more attractive for American and other foreign direct investors in industry. It provided a base for manufacturing inside the EEC. US companies regarded the fact that its workforce was English-speaking as another advantage. Low rates of corporation tax, compatible with EEC/EU law, have continued to lure these investors. Today, the Republic of Ireland has a thriving knowledge-based economy and its main industries include medical devices, computer hardware, software, pharmaceuticals and financial services.

Unlike the Republic, the UK did not hold a referendum before joining the EEC. But in 1974 the British Labour Party came to power under Prime Minister Harold Wilson, replacing the Conservative government of Ted Heath. In 1975 Wilson delivered on Labour's manifesto promise to hold a referendum in order to gauge support for continuing UK membership. The British voted 2:1 in favour of membership, which was a relief to the Irish government. In Northern Ireland the result was much closer than in England, Scotland or Wales, being 52:48 in favour. Wilson had laid the ground for success at negotiations with other European heads of state in Dublin.

Away from high politics normal life continued. The Summer Olympics at Munich in 1972 were marred by the political murder of participating Israelis. But they also provided a bright moment for Northern Ireland, which knew only too well its own violent outrages. Mary Peters won a gold medal in the women's pentathlon. She was participating as part of the UK contingent from Great Britain and Northern Ireland, with the island of Ireland divided at the Olympics as it is in politics. Northern Ireland was to receive its only other Olympic gold medals in 1988, when Stephen Martin and Jimmy Kirkwood won them as members of the UK hockey team in Seoul. Martin later became Deputy Chief Executive Officer (CEO) of the British Olympic Association, and then CEO of the Olympic Council of Ireland (in the Republic) from 2006 to 2017. Thus can sport transcend borders.

The Irish constitution of 1937 may be changed only by a referendum organised by the government. On 7 December 1972 citizens of the Republic voted 84:16 to remove from that constitution an original provision recognising 'the special position of the Holy Catholic Apostolic and Roman Church as the guardian of the Faith professed by the great majority of the citizens'. Although the provision had no known practical application, it was seen as outdated and potentially divisive. On the same day voters reduced the voting age from 21 to 18, as the United Kingdom parliament had already done by statute in 1969.

The Republic of Ireland was late in abolishing its legal requirement that women in certain public service jobs resign from employment when they married. European countries including Germany, the Netherlands and the UK had removed similar discriminatory provisions years earlier, although the UK retained a bar on married women in its foreign diplomatic service until 1973. Across the Republic into the 1970s, a marriage bar was widespread in practice in both the public and private sectors. It reflected a Catholic ethos concerning the place of women in the home. In 1973, influenced by the EEC, the Irish state abolished its marriage bar within the civil service. Other public bodies soon did so too. The reform did not include a right to reinstatement. The abolition of the bar was in line with a report from a commission on the status of women set up in 1970 by the Irish government. That report is seen as a milestone on the road to women's empowerment in Ireland, and the abolition of the marriage bar from 1973 is one of the principal reasons why many people in Ireland came to regard membership of the EEC/EU as liberating. The availability of married women in the workforce also facilitated economic expansion generally.

As efforts continued to resolve conflict in Northern Ireland, the UK and Irish governments met with nationalist and unionist parties at Sunningdale, England, in December 1973. It was the first such tripartite meeting since the 1920s. Participants agreed to set up a new form of devolved government in Northern Ireland, one intended to involve executive power-sharing between representatives of both sides of the community divide. The Irish government was party to the agreement, insistent by then (as it still is) that it has a stake on behalf of Irish people in any arrangement maintaining Northern Ireland in the United Kingdom. A Council of Ireland was also intended to function under the agreement, with limited powers to agree minor all-Ireland measures.

The Sunningdale agreement and its power-sharing executive were soon undermined by fierce unionist resistance. This included across the province in May 1974 the Ulster Workers' Council strike, involving the erection of barricades and other forms of intimidation that British authorities did not confront and face down: 'A million British citizens, the Protestants of Northern Ireland, staged what amounted to a rebellion against the Crown and won,' wrote Robert Fisk in his 1975 book on the strike. The centrality of the striking workers' control over power stations was highlighted by Joe Brydon in his 2020 book *1974–A World in Flux*. The collapse of the Northern Ireland executive then was a major blow to hopes for peace. Efforts to establish a functioning power-sharing executive (a local cross-community government) were to continue to prove shaky, and at times impossible.

In the Republic the general election of 28 February 1973 reflected a growing desire for change and reform. Fianna Fáil, the centre-right populist party founded by Éamon de Valera (who opposed the Anglo-Irish Treaty in 1921), had held power most recently since 1957. This time the centre-right Fine Gael along with the third largest party then, centre-left Labour, agreed in advance to form a coalition government if they won enough seats. They did so, and a government emerged under the premiership of Fine Gael leader Liam Cosgrave and the deputy premiership of Labour leader Brendan Corish. After 1973, as voters became more volatile and their loyalty to the main parties was sorely strained, such coalitions became quite a usual and generally stable form of government.

The northern Troubles spilled over bloodily into the Republic on 17 May 1974. Thirty-three civilians and an unborn child were killed, and hundreds injured, when unionist/loyalist paramilitaries planted four car bombs in Dublin and Monaghan. The ostensible collusion of British security forces in these and other loyalist atrocities created strains between the Irish and British governments.

A happier moment came for the Republic, marking its place as a state in the world, when in 1975 for the first time it was its turn to assume the presidency of the EEC.

The Republic's first mosque opened in 1976, in Dublin. There were few Muslims in Ireland before 1970, with most of them students. However, as the Republic's economy began to improve and modernise, technological and other jobs attracted applicants from overseas. Many of those who came settled long-term in Ireland. Today there are more than fifty places of worship for Muslims on the island. In the census of 1991 there were 3,875 persons in the Republic who described themselves as Muslim. By 2016 there were 63,443, constituting the largest religious grouping after Catholics and members of the Church of Ireland (Anglicans).

In May 1977 the Irish Employment Equality Act was passed in Dublin. This made discrimination on the grounds of sex or marital status unlawful, with very limited exceptions.

The general election of June 1977 saw Fianna Fáil, under its leader Jack Lynch, return to power in the Republic with a clear majority. Significantly, having formed a government, Lynch stepped down as leader and on 11 December 1979 Charles Haughey succeeded him as both party leader and Ireland's *taoiseach* (prime minister). Haughey was a controversial figure, competent but corrupt. Socially sophisticated, he came to represent a more modern, slicker and economically ambitious Ireland. As a government minister he had reformed outdated succession laws and had also introduced a scheme of tax exemption for artists, writers and composers that, with modifications, still operates today and is admired internationally. Yet his government embarked on a spending spree, exacerbating inflationary pressures while failing to stimulate the economy. It sowed a bitter harvest that would be reaped in the 1980s by way of inflation, increased unemployment and emigration. Haughey served as *taoiseach* in 1979–81, March–December 1982, and 1987–92.

On 21 July 1976 the IRA killed the British ambassador to Ireland Christopher Ewart-Biggs and his secretary Judith Cooke in a landmine attack in Dublin. It was a particularly shocking assassination, but many other people were dying in political violence in Northern Ireland every month. The Women for Peace or 'Peace People' group was founded there in 1976, by Mairead Corrigan and Betty Williams with the support of Ciaran McKeown. The catalyst for its foundation was the death of three children of Corrigan's sister, hit by a car driven by a member of the Provisional IRA who had just been shot by the British Army. Williams was in the area when that shooting happened. The Peace People organised large marches demanding compromise, but the level of compromise necessary for a settlement to hold was not yet forthcoming. For their efforts, Corrigan and Williams were awarded the Nobel Peace Prize in 1978. The Peace People movement lost momentum in the face of continuing atrocities and violence, and Corrigan went on to engage in activism against policies of the US, Israeli and other governments internationally. By a curious twist, the only Irish person to have previously won the Nobel Peace Prize was the lawyer Seán MacBride, who had been the IRA's chief-of-staff in 1936–37. He shared it in 1974, when recently elected UN Commissioner for Namibia, for his efforts on behalf of human rights. He played a leading role in setting up Amnesty International. In 1977 he was awarded the Lenin Peace Prize by the Soviet Union.

Atrocities came thick and fast in Northern Ireland in the 1970s. Among the worst was the La Mon House Hotel bombing by the Provisional IRA in 1978. 'Twelve people - seven men and five women, all Protestants - died in horrific circumstances, burned in a massive fireball. They were attending the annual dinner dance of a dog club. Thirty more were injured,' recalled the *Irish Times* later (21 Feb. 1998). It was said to be the highest death toll from an explosion since loyalists bombed McGurk's bar in north Belfast in 1971, killing fifteen people. And so it went, with two of the most significant attacks on the same day in August 1979 when the IRA killed eighteen British soldiers at Warrenpoint in Co. Down, and killed Lord Louis Mountbatten – cousin to Queen Elizabeth II – along with three other civilians in a bomb explosion on a small fishing boat he was using on vacation in the Republic. In 2015 Prince Charles, at the site of Mountbatten's death, said 'For me, Lord Mountbatten represented the grandfather I never had. It seemed as if the foundation of all that we held dear in life had been torn apart irreparably.' Many people in Northern Ireland knew that feeling. The IRA's reckless use of car bombs cost much civilian suffering, at little risk to those responsible. And loyalist gangs grabbed innocent Catholics off the street before torturing and killing them.

A Pope had never visited Ireland before John Paul II came in September 1979. He arrived just one month after the murder of Lord Mountbatten. His first speech on Irish soil, at Drogheda town in the Republic, near the border with Northern Ireland, included a powerful and sustained appeal to paramilitaries. Among other things he said, 'On my knees I beg you to turn away from the path of violence and to return to the ways of peace. You may claim to seek justice. All should believe in justice and seek justice, but violence only delays the day of justice.' Each of the main Christian churches in Ireland has remained an all-island administrative unit since partition in 1920, but some Protestants advised Pope John Paul not to set foot in Northern Ireland. He did not do so. The Pope's visit was significant because he made a clear statement of the Catholic Church's opposition to tactics used by the IRA. This helped the government of the Republic to isolate violent nationalists.

The Pope's visit was also remarkable because of the vast number of citizens who turned out to welcome him at each venue. This was a manifestation of deep historical connections between his Church and the great majority of Irish people, who have a Catholic ancestry, and of the long-held respect among Irish Catholics for a Church that supported them for centuries through extreme poverty, repression and famine. Yet if the Irish bishops thought that the papal visit would result in a revival of their Church's pre-eminence in Ireland, which was already fading, they were greatly mistaken. What might have been seen as a moment of triumph, or even triumphalism, may be regarded in hindsight as largely a public vote of thanks to the Catholic Church for all that it had done. The future was another matter.

At a ceremony in Galway for the Pope, which was intended to inspire young people to be loyal to the Catholic Church, the principal masters of ceremony were a populist priest Michael Cleary and a respected bishop Eamonn Casey. It later transpired that each had fathered at least one child and each had treated his child's mother shoddily. These and worse scandals were soon to shatter people's trust in the institution of the church, which seemed incapable of responding adequately.

It was only in 1979 that an Irish government amended the law to permit even the limited importation and sale of contraceptives in the Republic of Ireland. In 1971, in a celebrated publicity stunt, a group of feminists had highlighted opposition to the old law by going from Dublin to Belfast to buy condoms, and returning on the next train to Dublin to embarrass the authorities amid a blaze of publicity. In 1974 an effort by the Fine Gael/Labour coalition to liberalise the law had failed bizarrely when *Taoiseach* Liam Cosgrave and others voted against a proposal introduced by their own government's minister for justice. The 1979 change was engineered by the Fianna Fáil government of *Taoiseach* Charles Haughey, who in a memorable phrase described his Health (Family Planning) Act as 'an Irish solution to an Irish problem'. It now permitted contraceptives to be sold to those seeking them 'for the purpose, *bona fide* [in good faith] of family planning', a phrase that some took to mean married couples but that might include others. No one had to produce a marriage certificate when buying condoms, and doctors might continue to prescribe the pill as simply a 'cycle regulator' as they were doing already. The married Haughey himself had long had a mistress. Further liberalisation in the years ahead saw the remaining Irish anti-contraceptive laws and other legal measures once supportive of the teaching of the Catholic Church swept away. Condoms are now on sale to all adults in pharmacies and supermarkets.

A symbolic moment for the Republic came in 1979 when it broke the long-standing fixed link between the value of its pound and UK sterling, with the Republic now joining the new European Monetary System. The

EMS was created to achieve currency stability across Europe, through the co-ordination of monetary policy. The United Kingdom was the only EEC member not to join the EMS. However, even as aspects of Irish society changed, an underlying conservatism constantly reasserted itself. An example of this was the frustration of even a minor reform in respect to the Irish senate. The Republic's constitution made provision for graduates of the state's then existing universities to elect six members of the upper house. Although people overwhelmingly voted 9:1 in a referendum on 5 July 1979 to permit *Dáil Éireann* to extend the franchise to newer educational institutions, by early 2023 its deputies still had not done so.

In 1979 Van Morrison, one of Northern Ireland's best-known singers and songwriters, injected a little optimism into life with what many consider to be his best hit, 'Bright Side of the Road'. It is on his album *Into the Music*. Shakira later gave the song a memorable rendition at Barack Obama's first Inaugural Neighborhood Ball in Washington, in January 2009. Among other Irish singers and musicians to enjoy international success have been Enya, The Dubliners, The Chieftains, Bono of U2, Phil Lynott with Thin Lizzy, Christy Moore, The Undertones, Sinéad O'Connor, Hozier, Nadine Coyle, Westlife, The Corrs and The Cranberries.

Set-Backs: 1980–1989

The decade of the 1980s was disappointing, with high inflation and recession, unemployment and renewed emigration. Although the economic fortunes of the Republic of Ireland have been turned around radically for the better since 1961, the process of recovery and growth has not been constant. Easier access to education and generous tax breaks for foreign multinational companies were not enough. However, over time, the exodus from labour-intensive agriculture and other low-productivity sectors was absorbed by new jobs in Ireland, many of which were highly specialised when it came to the technology involved. Not only did young Irish people find work with advanced employers such as Intel – which began its Irish operations in 1989 – but a growing spirit of Irish entrepreneurship found expression through new native companies.

Cultural activities benefited from economic improvements. In 1980 the Irish government belatedly set up a state-funded Irish film board (Bord Scannán na hÉireann, now Fís Éireann/Screen Ireland). Tax incentives were boosted for film production. The number of Irish films and co-productions with broad appeal has greatly increased since then, including *My Left Foot* (1989) *The Field* (1990), *Adam & Paul* (2003),*The Wind That Shakes the Barley* (2006), *Garage* (2007), *Kings* (2007) and *An Cailín Ciúin* ('*The Quiet Girl*', 2022). The latter became the first Irish-language movie nominated for an Oscar in the International Feature Film category. It did not win but, also in 2023, Northern Ireland's *An Irish Goodbye* won the Oscar for best live action short film. Prominent Irish and British-Irish filmmakers include Jim Sheridan, Terry George, Neil Jordan and Martin McDonagh.

It was in 1980 too that the Ulster playwright Brian Friel founded with actor Stephen Rea the Field Day Theatre Company in Northern Ireland's deeply divided Derry/Londonderry city. With the collaboration of poet Seamus Heaney and playwright Tom Kilroy among others, Field Day became a popular project that created an intellectual space in which to explore Irish identities. Friel himself had been on the civil rights march in Derry on Bloody Sunday 1972. His best-known plays include *Philadelphia Here I Come*, *Translations* and *Dancing at Lughnasa* – the latter winning Tony Awards and being made into a film starring Meryl Streep. By 2002 Field Day had also published the five volumes of its *Anthology of Irish Writing*, edited by Seamus Deane. Other Ulster dramatists who have explored the question of identity as well as class on the island include Frank McGuinness, whose play *Observe the Sons of Ulster Marching Towards the Somme* (about unionists in the British Army) premiered at Dublin's Abbey Theatre in 1985.

North of the Irish border in the 1980s, there seemed to be no end to political and paramilitary conflict. But in the Republic a new model of social partnership contributed to a remarkable recovery and to the state becoming in the 1990s one of the fastest growing economies in the EU or the OECD. Today, the population of the Republic has recovered to levels not seen since the mid-1800s.

Margaret Thatcher played a big role in Irish affairs throughout the 1980s, as violence continued in Northern Ireland. Becoming UK prime minister in 1979, she was re-elected in 1983 and 1987. In 1981, she claimed Northern Ireland was 'as British as Finchley' – which was her parliamentary constituency in the south of England. Many Irish found her statement ludicrous. Thatcher's steely determination was evident during the hunger strike by republican prisoners in 1981, and unionists admired it. But her hard-line attitude did not end the Northern Ireland Troubles, and she was to understand eventually that British suppression alone could not achieve a settled peace in Ireland. It was bound to fail, as it had failed in the past.

Irish prisoners had previously used the hunger strike as a means of protest and propaganda, perhaps most notably when Terence MacSwiney died in Brixton prison in England in 1920. A republican, he had been elected lord mayor of Cork city in Ireland before his arrest during the Irish War of Independence. There was also a broader cultural context, which the British may not have fully appreciated when planning their response in 1981. In older Gaelic culture fasting against someone for a debt or other purpose could cause them lasting public disgrace and damage.

The hunger strikers 'failed' to achieve their demands in 1981. But London won what was in effect a 'Pyrrhic' or deceptive victory. For Thatcher's apparent success hardened the determination of even moderate nationalists north and south of the border to ensure the reform of Northern Ireland.

The immediate purpose of the hunger strikes in Northern Ireland in 1981 and 1982 was to protest once more against the UK government's decision in 1976 to refuse special category status to those convicted of paramilitary offences after that date. Such prisoners had previously been granted it. The prisoners did not regard themselves as ordinary criminals and resented attempts to force them to wear prison uniforms or to do work assigned by prison authorities. They also demanded the right to associate freely and to organise their own educational and recreational activities. Most such prisoners were housed in buildings known as 'Hblocks', at the prison complex near Lisburn known as both Long Kesh and The Maze. Prisoners had earlier campaigned for the restoration of special category status by means of a 'blanket protest'. They wrapped their bedclothes around themselves rather than don a uniform. This then became the 'dirty protest' when they refused to wash, and they also daubed their own cells with excrement. In 1980 a number of the prisoners went on hunger strike, but stopped after seven weeks. However, the hunger strike that began in 1981 was more determined, resulting in the death by starvation of ten men. Of these the best known was Bobby Sands, who had been elected a member of the UK parliament while on hunger strike. Following his death the UK government passed a law preventing people while imprisoned for more than a year standing for parliament, and thus stopped other hunger strikers from becoming MPs. In Steve McQueen's *Hunger*, an award-winning 2008 film about the events of 1981, Michael Fassbender acted the role of Sands.

The hunger strike was eventually called off, by which time the unbending attitude of the British government had angered most nationalists north and south of the border. The manner in which Thatcher's government handled the matter was a reminder of old imperialist arrogance and of the fact that Britain had allowed Northern Ireland to be governed unfairly for too long. Thatcher's approach affronted *Taoiseach* Charles Haughey, and their relations sank even lower when his government subsequently decided not to support British sanctions against Argentina during the Falklands War in 1982. The British response to the hunger strikes was partly responsible for the rise of Provisional Sinn Féin as a political force on the island of Ireland.

The fact that Bobby Sands had been elected to parliament while on hunger strike encouraged the strategic use of political participation by hard-line republicans, while horrifying unionists. Danny Morrison, then the publicity officer of Provisional Sinn Féin, infamously asked delegates at his party's annual conference (its *'ard fheis'*) in Dublin later that year, 'Who here really believes we can win the war through the ballot box?' In the silence that followed, he added to applause, 'But will anyone here object if, with a ballot paper in this hand, and an Armalite in this hand, we take power in Ireland?' (*Irish Times*, 2 Nov. 1981, page 7). The Armalite rifle was then a preferred weapon of the Provisional IRA and many still see Morrison's statement as an indication of underlying ambiguity on the part of Sinn Féin as regards not merely using but also upholding democracy on both sides of the Irish border. In 1983 IRA personnel 'kidnapped' Shergar, a famous and successful racehorse. Their ransom plan went wrong and Shergar is believed to have been killed.

During 1981 and 1982 there were three general elections in the Republic of Ireland. Charles Haughey lost his centre-right Fianna Fáil majority twice to the other main parties which were the centre-right Fine Gael under Garret Fitzgerald and its smaller Labour Party coalition partner. Haughey had been kept in power for a while by a leftist, inner-city independent deputy Tony Gregory and by the small leftist Workers' Party, to whom he had first made specific promises. Critics on each side regarded this as a pact with the devil, and the arrangement collapsed when Haughey introduced significant cuts in public spending. Greater political stability returned to the Republic when a new Fine Gael/Labour coalition government was formed in 1982 and remained in office until 1987.

Abortion had been criminalised throughout Britain and Ireland in 1861, by the parliament of the United Kingdom, but was legalised in Britain in 1967. In 1983 a bitterly fought referendum in the Republic saw voters reinforce the 1861 ban by agreeing to insert a new provision into the constitution affirming it, even as many Irish women now went to Britain for abortions. This 'eighth amendment' allowed just one exception – where a mother's life was in imminent danger for medical reasons an abortion might be carried out in Ireland. In 1992 the infamous 'X-case' (below) would see the implications of that exception teased out. The provision passed in 1983 would be repealed in 2018.

On 12 October 1984 the Provisional IRA tried to kill Margaret Thatcher and members of her cabinet when it bombed the Grand Hotel in Brighton, England, where her Conservative Party was holding its annual conference. She escaped injury but five people died and dozens were injured.

In early 1984 media reported shocking events that reflected attitudes towards unmarried mothers and babies in Ireland. In Granard, Co. Longford, schoolboys found Ann Lovett dying. She was just fifteen years old. Beside her, at a little grotto built to honour Mary, mother of Jesus, lay a stillborn baby boy. Ashamed and frightened, she had concealed her pregnancy and had tried to deliver the baby on her own. She had with her scissors to cut the umbilical cord. Three months later, further south, began the 'Kerry Babies' fiasco. One of two dead babies found in Co. Kerry, at Cahirciveen, had been stabbed repeatedly and the other, at Tralee, battered. The subsequent police (garda) investigation was botched, and an official tribunal of enquiry satisfied few. The private sexual history of one leading suspect, Joanne Hayes, became a matter of public knowledge and curiosity. She later received financial compensation for her treatment. New arrests in the case were made as recently as March 2023. These events, along with scandals about mother and baby homes and other institutions into the late twentieth century, revealed attitudes and behaviour towards pregnant women and babies that are regarded as shameful today. Today unmarried cohabitation and the birth of children outside marriage are common and are unlikely to cause great community upset. The provision of contraception and abortion, and improved services for women in distress, have helped to create a better (if far from perfect) social context. Ireland has also ceased to be a predominantly rural society, and the influence of a conservative and judgmental Irish Catholic Church has waned even as that Church itself became more compassionate.

In June 1984 Ronald Reagan became the third sitting US president to visit Ireland. The first had been John Fitzgerald Kennedy, on a remarkable visit in June 1963. JFK's trip resonated with the Irish public. It was a reminder that a century of emigration had resulted in better if sometimes lonely economic prospects abroad for many who left Ireland – including for JFK's ancestor Patrick Kennedy from Co. Wexford. In 1963, it was only two years since the population of the Republic had reached its lowest point since the Great Famine of the 1840s. Departing from Shannon Airport, named after Ireland's longest river nearby, JFK told well-wishers 'I'm going to come back and see old Shannon's face again.' He never did, being assassinated in Dallas a few months later.

Cynics said that visits to Ireland by US presidents, which became more common than those to many bigger countries, were of mutual benefit. US politicians were seen to be honouring Irish-American voters, and Irish politicians could use the visits as a platform from which to encourage the inward investment from the United States that was helping Ireland to prosper.

Improvements in air transportation were very helpful to an island such as Ireland, eager to keep in touch with emigrants and their descendants, while also building business networks around the globe. From the 1980s to the 2020s Ryanair rose rapidly to become the largest international airline carrying passengers outside the USA. This success epitomised fundamental changes that have taken place in the ideology of independent Ireland during the past fifty years. Providing first a modest service between the rural Irish city of Waterford and Gatwick in London in July 1985, Ryanair took its name from that of the family of its founder Tony Ryan. Its creation reflected the outward-looking ambition and entrepreneurial spirit of new Irish businesses in the second-half of the twentieth century. It became a by-word for brashness under its long-term chief executive Michael O'Leary. Educated at an upper middle-class Jesuit boarding school, O'Leary assumed a blunt 'man-in-the-street' style persona that offended and delighted the public in equal measure. Ryanair expanded rapidly across Europe by offering low-cost flights to many destinations, frequently using small airports that previously had little business. His pugnacious attitude towards regulators and unions and his unapologetic no-frills service for customers did not stop increasing numbers of people from flying Ryanair. Citizens might tut-tut about O'Leary's manner, but they seemed willing to tolerate it for the value and convenience that came with it. The state-owned Aer Lingus had long been 'the Irish airline'. There was a national pride in its appearance and style. It had long felt to Irish people and tourists as if they were already in Ireland as soon as they stepped on board an Aer Lingus aircraft in a foreign city. But it was not low-cost, and its ambition for new routes was limited. If Aer Lingus had been seen as 'the flag-carrier' for Ireland, its signature logo of a three-leafed Irish shamrock was now matched by an Irish harp on Ryanair planes. The Irish government later privatised Aer Lingus, with Ryanair acquiring a significant minority stake in the company. Aer Lingus is now a wholly-owned subsidiary of IAG, which also owns British Airways and Iberia.

On 15 November 1985, at Hillsborough Castle in Co. Down, Prime Minister Margaret Thatcher and *Taoiseach* Garret Fitzgerald signed an Anglo-Irish agreement that acknowledged an advisory role for the government of the Republic of Ireland in Northern Ireland's affairs, one that many unionists found potentially intrusive. At the same time, Dublin officially acknowledged what had always been its position in practice since the partition of the island, namely that there would be no change in the constitutional status of Northern Ireland without the consent of a majority of its people. In other words, Irish political unity will happen only if a majority of people in Northern Ireland agrees to it. This is despite the fact that partition was forced on Ireland against the clear wishes of a majority of its people as expressed at the UK general election of 1918 and otherwise. While the Provisional IRA and its Sinn Féin political wing dismissed the agreement of 1985, more moderate parties hoped that it might signal a successful devolved government in Northern Ireland and a greater level of trust between the two sides. In fact, in hindsight, it achieved less than was hoped at the time. But in respect to co-operation between the Irish and British governments as regards security and legal affairs and cross-border co-operation, it created a somewhat better relationship.

Following the 1985 agreement, the UK and Irish governments - supported financially by the European Community, the US government, Canada, Australia and New Zealand - set up the International Fund for Ireland, to support investment that would encourage contact between unionists and nationalists across the Irish border. It has supported over 6,000 projects in Ireland and is seen as a success. Substantial investment has also come to Ireland from The Atlantic Philanthropies, a fund set up by modest US billionaire Chuck Feeney who decided in 1982 to devote his enormous wealth to the service of humanity. His ancestors came from Co. Fermanagh, in what is today Northern Ireland.

Ireland may have been liberalising economically, but it could still be very conservative in its social attitudes. In June 1986 voters rejected a proposal to remove from the Republic's constitution of 1937 its blanket ban on divorce. Few guessed just how soon that decision would be reversed.

In November 1986 Provisional Sinn Féin decided to end its abstentionist policy of not participating in *Dáil Éireann*, which body it had previously scorned. Since 1986 its representation in the Republic's parliament has steadily grown. The party's gradual shift towards constitutional politics was also signalled north of the border when the leading constitutional nationalist and SDLP leader John Hume and Sinn Féin's president Gerry Adams met for discussions. These talks became a major impetus to the 'Peace Process' that led to the Belfast/Good Friday Agreement of 1998.

From 1980 to 1987 living standards in the Republic fell. Unemployment soared, from 7% in 1979 to nearly 18% in 1987. Inflation and the growth in jobless numbers saw emigration return as a common option for young people. It was a real setback. But now, building on strands in the 'National Understanding' of the later 1970s and early 1980s, employers, unions and the farming organisations all signed up to the first Programme for National Recovery (PNR). It came into effect on 1 January 1987. Known as the three 'pillars', these three groups had been coaxed by the government into finding a novel way of working together for wage restraint, taxation reform, industrial growth and greater social justice. The Programme for National Recovery of 1987-1990 was a binding agreement on wage levels in the public and private sectors. It involved trade union support for a tightening of public expenditure in return for the government maintaining the value of social welfare payments and reforming the income tax system. The ordinary public whose taxation was deducted at source from their salaries (the 'Pay As You Earn' system) had begun to take to the streets in large numbers to protest at levels of taxation and at tax evasion by the self-employed. The PNR worked so well that the groups involved agreed to continue their partnership throughout the 1990s. Their agreement laid the foundation for the phenomenal boom in Ireland's fortunes that transformed the Republic of Ireland into the 'Celtic Tiger'.

The Republic's general elections of 1987 and 1989 saw the controversial Charles Haughey of Fianna Fáil back in power. He held on as *taoiseach* until early 1992. In a crisis over public finances, Labour had withdrawn from its coalition with Fine Gael and so cleared the way for Haughey to return. *Dáil Éireann* was gradually becoming more fragmented. A new right-of-centre party, the Progressive Democrats, now pushed Labour into fourth place and gave Haughey the support he needed to govern.

Between 1988 and 1991 Haughey received substantial sums of money from the big businessman Ben Dunne (of Dunnes Stores), who contributed about £200,000 to the Fine Gael party too. During the 1980s Haughey as *taoiseach* also had knowledge of the phone-tapping of three senior journalists whose conversations were intercepted by gardaí (police) on behalf of the government. When this became known publicly, he resigned and the journalists later received compensation. He was widely regarded as cavalier and arrogant, a 'strong man' who had his admirers despite (or perhaps because of) his sins and who set the tone for bullish economic expansion. Emblematic of his persona was the revelation that in 1991 he spent almost £16,000 of public money on shirts from the exclusive French company Charvet, and had them transported to Ireland in the diplomatic bags of the Irish embassy in France.

On 26 May 1987 the Republic held a referendum on the Single European Act. Seventy percent of the electorate voted in favour of the measure which extended the powers, internal free market and cohesion of the EEC (now EU). The result underlined the strength of support in Ireland for membership of the European community. The UK was later to leave the Single Market as part of Brexit, against the wishes of a majority of people in Northern Ireland, but under a Brexit protocol Northern Ireland was then to remain aligned with the Single Market to avoid the necessity of a hard customs border being re-erected on the island of Ireland.

The history of Northern Ireland in the late twentieth century was a catalogue of atrocities, a list of horrible sectarian and other political murders. One of these was the killing of Patrick Finucane, a Catholic solicitor who had represented nationalist activists and paramilitaries. On 12 February 1989 he was shot dead in front of his family. In a special report, fourteen years later, Deputy Commissioner John Stevens of the London Metropolitan Police concluded that members of the UK security forces had colluded with loyalist paramilitaries in the murder.

On 8 November 1987 one of the most awful IRA bombings occurred during a ceremony in Enniskillen. It was Remembrance Day, when people throughout the United Kingdom wear poppies to recall soldiers killed in its wars. An IRA bomb exploded at a memorial in the centre of the Co. Fermanagh town, killing eleven people and injuring dozens. Gordon Wilson, who was present with his daughter when she died there, later became a public example of Christian forgiveness and was subsequently appointed to the *Seanad* (senate) of the Republic of Ireland. Six months earlier the British SAS had ambushed and killed eight IRA members engaged in an attack on a police station at Loughgall, Co. Armagh. If the IRA regarded its Enniskillen attack as some kind of revenge for Loughgall, the vast majority of nationalists and republicans throughout Ireland were revolted by the action. Subsequent attempts to depict the bombing as a bungled attack intended to kill security forces were unconvincing. North and south of the Irish border, such events alienated potential voters for Sinn Féin. When in 1988 the Republic belatedly passed legislation to permit the licensing of commercial radio and television stations in competition with the state-owned RTE, it extended to these an existing ban ('Section 31') on interviewing spokespeople for certain listed paramilitary organisations including Sinn Féin/IRA and its unionist equivalents. The UK adopted a similar ban.

Meanwhile, in July 1987, Stephen Roche had become the first Irish cyclist to win the Tour de France. Between 1978 and 1982, the popular Seán Kelly had won stages of that competition and attracted Irish interest in it. *Taoiseach* Charles Haughey cashed in on the interest by going to Paris and ensuring that he was included in photographs alongside the victorious Roche. Critics saw this as a cynical stunt, not least because Irish governments had an unimpressive record in relation to the funding and support of minority sports.

Birth of the Celtic Tiger: 1990–1999
During the 1990s, the Republic of Ireland enjoyed spectacular economic growth and came to be spoken of in the same awed terms as Asian 'tiger' economies. Despite earlier setbacks, an underlying upward trend in the Republic's financial fortunes since the 1960s now resumed. In 2010 the governor of the Central Bank of Ireland, Patrick Honohan, said, 'New business-like working methods and a respect for the discipline of the market percolated through the economy from the wave of US and other multinational companies who found Ireland a profitable productive base.'

From 1988 to 2007 the Republic's Gross Domestic Product expanded by six per cent per annum on average (reaching double digits on average during 1995-2000). Even more astonishing, the unemployment rate shrank from sixteen per cent in 1994 to four per cent in 2000, which effectively was full employment for the first time in modern Irish history. Non-agricultural employment jumped from one third of the population in 1993 to almost half in 2007. But not everyone benefited equally from the boom, and chances were lost to put in place timely systematic reforms of social services, to reform political processes and to build the best possible infrastructure in health, housing and education.

The new decade started on a positive note. Thirty years later the *Irish Examiner* would correctly describe it as 'an unforgettable summer that still leaves us smiling'. The World Cup of June 1990 was simply great fun for people in the Republic, most of whom watched at least some of it on TV and quite a few of whom travelled to see their soccer team play. The team was managed by the former English international player Jack Charlton. It was the first time that the Republic had got beyond the qualifying rounds. It now reached the quarter-finals, doing so without actually winning a single match within the normal ninety minutes. Through the 1990s the team rode a wave of relative success for a small country. Unlike in rugby, there are separate soccer teams on each side of the Irish border. Northern Ireland's team has also qualified for the World Cup finals, in 1958 (when it reached the quarter finals), 1982 and 1986.

The Republic was increasingly self-confident and optimistic. There was a newly discovered pride in Ireland's emigrants (or its 'diaspora' as they now became known). One focus of popular affection on the Republic's soccer team was Paul McGrath, born in Middlesex to a Nigerian father who met his Irish mother during medical studies in Dublin. 'Ooh, Aah, Paul McGrath!' and 'Olé! Olé! Olé!' became unlikely crowd chants heard at the stadiums where the Republic's team played – and wherever Irish people gathered to watch matches in 1990 and in the subsequent World Cups of 1994 and 2002 for which the Republic also qualified. When Glasgow-born Ray Houghton scored the only and spectacular goal to give Ireland victory against Italy at the Giants Stadium in New Jersey in 1994, it was a moment of ecstasy for Irish supporters.

The liberal Mary Robinson was elected President of Ireland in 1990, beating the favourite Brian Lenihan (*left*), to the disgust of his party leader and Ireland's *Taoiseach* Charles Haughey (*right*). *Courtesy National Library of Ireland.*

Another sign of change in the Republic was the election of liberal candidate Mary Robinson as president in December 1990. Robinson, a civil rights and women's rights lawyer, had long been a thorn in the side of the Irish establishment. Nominated as president by the small Irish

Labour Party, she beat a strong favourite, the usually canny Brian Lenihan of Fianna Fáil. He was caught out in a lie about a past political episode. He was also damaged by a ministerial colleague snidely remarking of Robinson that during the campaign she had discovered a 'new-found interest in her family'. When president, Robinson lit a lamp permanently in an upstairs window of her official residence in Dublin's Phoenix Park to let members of the Irish diaspora know that they are always welcome back in Ireland. In late 1997 she became the United Nations High Commissioner for Human Rights.

When the Republic of Ireland's successful first Programme for National Recovery (1987–1990) expired, the social partnership at its heart was renewed on 1 January 1991 by the 'Programme for Economic and Social Progress' (PESP), which ran from 1991 to 1993. Similar agreements followed until 2005. These were music to the ears of economists and politicians, and became the signature tune of prosperity to people generally in the Republic. Irish governments later pointed out that during the first four programmes alone, from 1987 to 2000, economic growth was greater than twice the EU average, inflation fell to one of the lowest rates in the EU, and employment in the private non-agricultural sector showed an annual average growth of about 2.5%. Budgetary consolidation measures linked to the programmes gave Ireland's government one of the lowest financial deficits in the EU.

While there was broad political and social support for the partnership arrangement, there were also sceptics and critics. Some employers deeply resented trade unions having a direct influence on the determination of how business might or might not be conducted, while some workers thought that the unions were being 'co-opted' into an economic model founded on conservative principles that was more beneficial to those with 'permanent' jobs than to casual and contract labour. Some voluntary organisations likewise suspected that the deals were better for workers in employment, including trade union officials, than for the marginalised and unemployed. Groups interested in global issues worried that Ireland was throwing in its lot with the rich countries of the European Union, sharing wealth rather than redistributing it across the world. But most citizens were pleased to see their standard of living rise. They were happy to ride on the 'Celtic Tiger'. Lone voices warned of the dangers of getting carried away by euphoria, of forgetting that pride often comes before a fall. They were ignored.

One sign of a gradually maturing economy was the establishment of the Irish Museum of Modern Art in 1990, in an historic seventeenth century complex that had been long neglected. This was the former Royal Hospital Kilmainham, once sister institution of the Royal Hospital Chelsea, London. Painters such as Jack B. Yeats, Harry Clarke and Mainie Jellett set a standard for Irish artists in the new state after independence, but many struggled to make a living. Jellett and Evie Hone were among a small group who founded the Irish Exhibition of Living Art (IELA) in 1943 as a platform for fresh ideas. In 1972 the original IELA management handed over to a new generation. Among well-known Irish artists in recent decades have been Louis le Brocquy, Mary Swanzy, Tony O'Malley, Robert Ballagh, Brian Bourke, Markey Robinson, Patrick Hickey, Mick O'Dea and Pauline Bewick. Francis Bacon and Sean Scully were both born in Dublin, but moved abroad. Bacon's heir donated the artist's legendary and chaotic London studio and its 7,000 objects to the Hugh Lane Gallery in

Dublin, where it is reconstructed in archaeological detail on permanent display.

Growing wealth exacerbated financial temptations. One scandal came to light when a British ITV programme of 13 May 1991 highlighted Ireland's beef processing industry. This led to *Dáil Éireann* establishing a tribunal of investigation. Various official enquiries set up by government then and later have bred cynicism by their perceived insignificance relative to levels of ostensible wrongdoing by business, banking, church and state. When corruption in local government in Dublin could no longer be ignored, for example, it was partly investigated. Yet other local authorities nationally remained unexamined regardless of suspicions. The cost and duration of investigations have also raised questions about the efficiency and will of the independent Irish state.

In 1992 Charles Haughey resigned as *taoiseach* and was replaced as leader of his party and government by Albert Reynolds. The whiff of controversy and corruption around Haughey had simply got too strong. Both Haughey and Reynolds, for example, had relationships with Saddam Hussein's Iraq that were not transparent. Another prominent politician, Ray Burke, minister for communications in Haughey's government, was later jailed for evading tax on payments made to him while minister by the backers of a commercial radio station. He also took money from building developers. A chance was then lost to root out more robustly any political corruption at local and national level in Ireland. There have been few convictions for financial corruption in the state.

In 1992, too, evidence emerged that drug abuse and dependency was becoming a serious social issue. The leading businessman Ben Dunne was charged in Florida with possession of cocaine, and after a high-profile trial was ordered to spend a month in a rehabilitation clinic in England.

On 5 March 1992, in a major legal case that rocked the Republic and generated much detailed debate about abortion, the High Court granted an order preventing a fourteen-year-old rape victim from leaving Ireland when it became known that she intended to have her pregnancy terminated in Britain (where abortion was legal). Because the identity of the girl was protected due to her age, this became known as the 'X-case'. It concerned the wording of the abortion ban inserted by amendment in the Irish constitution in 1983. The Supreme Court now decided on appeal that a citizen could not be deprived of the right to travel in circumstances such as those of X. The court found that the single exception allowing abortion, where a woman's life is in danger, applied when there was evidence of the real danger of her committing suicide. Later, the rapist of girl X was sentenced to just four years in jail. Following his release, he was in 1999 imprisoned for the sexual assault of another under-age girl.

In May 1992 the respect in which Irish people long held the Catholic Church was dealt a blow. It was revealed that the popular bishop of Galway, Eamonn Casey, had fathered a child by a young woman whose own father had sent her to the bishop for care and protection. When the news broke, the bishop fled to America. Unfolding sexual scandals within the Catholic Church had a special impact because Irish bishops had long condemned sexual sins in particular.

The Republic's general election of November 1992 continued a trend of fragmentation in Irish politics, as coalition or minority governments became and remained the norm in the Republic. The Labour Party did relatively well, winning an unprecedented thirty-three of the 166 seats.

Many assumed that it would join with Fine Gael to form a government but, instead, it supported the Fianna Fáil party that was led then by Albert Reynolds.

On the same day as the November general election, voters were presented with a referendum that reflected growing public awareness of the nuances of the debate around abortion. The public was being educated by having to inform itself in the face of fierce conflicting campaigns about the 'right to choose'. It would come eventually to decide that abortion be provided within Ireland. For now, it simply rejected a new proposal that would have tightened even further the state's already tight controls on abortion by *excluding* the real possibility of suicide from consideration in respect to the threat to a pregnant woman's life. This was then the sole permitted ground for abortion. Voters also endorsed the Supreme Court's judgment in the X-case by affirming the right to travel to another state for an abortion as well as the freedom to make available in the Republic information on abortion services lawfully available in other states. There were also other signs of growing liberalisation in the Republic, including legislation passed in June 1993 decriminalising homosexual acts. Within twenty-five years an openly gay man would become *taoiseach*/prime minister of the Republic.

In December 1993 the first of certain deposits was made to bank accounts held in the name of Bertie Ahern (the Irish government's then minister for finance and a future *taoiseach*) and to accounts held in the name of his daughters and his close friend Celia Larkin. *Taoiseach* Charles Haughey had appointed Ahern minister for finance in 1991, and Ahern infamously signed blank cheques for Haughey that were drawn on a Fianna Fáil account. A tribunal that *Dáil Éireann* established to inquire into planning matters and payments to politicians (the Flood/Mahon Tribunal, 1997–2012) was to find (paragraph 12.01) that 'Mr Ahern did not truthfully account for the origins of specific cash lodgments' in his own bank accounts between December 1993 and late 1995.

Another indication of problems in the Irish state came when a TV station delved deeply into the breaking scandal of paedophile Fr Brendan Smyth and the failure to extradite him from the Republic to Northern Ireland. Ulster Television's *Counterpoint* programme in October 1994 could be received widely within the Republic and it shocked Catholics across the island. Revelations about Smyth acted as a catalyst for further and deepening media coverage of child abuse, to which both church and state authorities failed to respond adequately.

In 1994, when the then coalition of Fianna Fáil and Labour collapsed in a row over the appointment of the president of the High Court, *Dáil Éireann* was not dissolved but instead took the unusual step of directly electing John Bruton of Fine Gael to form a new government with the support of others. In 1994 too, but on a distinctly lighter note, Ireland hosted yet another annual Eurovision song contest. With four victories in the 1990s, and seven wins overall, Ireland is still the most successful country in that contest along with Sweden. A short orchestral dance piece, broadcast during an interval in the finals in Dublin in 1994, delighted the television audience and became the basis of *Riverdance*, a full musical stage production that is still being performed internationally today. *Riverdance* is expressive of the mood of modern Ireland, bringing a new energy to traditional Irish dance and music.

On 24 November 1995, by a wafer-thin majority (0.5%), voters in the Republic opted to amend the constitution to permit divorce. The

Republic's marriage law was to be further liberalised in 2019 when more than 80% of voters elected to recognise foreign divorces and also to permit parliament to reduce the required waiting time for divorces.

One of the factors that has contributed to changing attitudes and increased confidence in the Republic has been the state's commitment to high levels of education, facilitated not least by government decisions to make access to second level education free to all from 1969 and then to abolish university tuition costs from 1996. Critics claim that governments since then have not invested adequately in education to compensate for the loss of fees.

In October 1995 the much-loved and respected Irish poet Seamus Heaney won the Nobel Prize in Literature. His sensitive poetry has universal appeal. A Catholic who was born in Northern Ireland, Heaney took up residence in the Republic but resisted simplistic political categorisation. Later that same year, on the first visit of any US president to Northern Ireland, Bill Clinton quoted lines by Heaney. It was the first of Clinton's three visits to Ireland while president. He took a personal interest in the peace process, maintaining pressure on both sides to reach a deal. Joe Biden came to quote the same lines by Heaney in his US presidential campaign in 2020:

> History says, Don't hope
> On this side of the grave.
> But then, once in a lifetime
> The longed-for tidal wave
> Of justice can rise up,
> And hope and history rhyme.

Accepting the Nobel Prize, Heaney told a poignant true story from the continuing Troubles:

> One of the most harrowing moments in the whole history of the harrowing of the heart in Northern Ireland came when a minibus full of workers being driven home one January evening in 1976 was held up by armed and masked men and the occupants of the van ordered at gunpoint to line up at the side of the road. Then one of the masked executioners said to them, 'Any Catholics among you, step out here'. As it happened, this particular group, with one exception, were all Protestants, so the presumption must have been that the masked men were Protestant paramilitaries about to carry out a tit-for-tat sectarian killing of the Catholic as the odd man out, the one who would have been presumed to be in sympathy with the IRA and all its actions. It was a terrible moment for him, caught between dread and witness, but he did make a motion to step forward. Then, the story goes, in that split second of decision, and in the relative cover of the winter evening darkness, he felt the hand of the Protestant worker next to him take his hand and squeeze it in a signal that said no, don't move, we'll not betray you, nobody need know what faith or party you belong to. All in vain, however, for the man stepped out of the line; but instead of finding a gun at his temple, he was thrown backward and away as the gunmen opened fire on those remaining in the line, for these were not Protestant terrorists, but members, presumably, of the Provisional IRA.

While Heaney and other poets responded in verse to the Troubles, novelists such as Brian Moore and Deirdre Madden also grappled with the theme. Joan Lingard's Young Adult novel *Across the Barricades* (about Kevin and Sadie) became a playscript for schools in Northern Ireland.

As political violence in Northern Ireland continued to horrify people, the Republic was shocked by a new kind of criminal violence. On 26 June 1996 Veronica Guerin, an investigative journalist with the *Sunday*

Independent (then the most popular Sunday paper across all social classes in Ireland), was shot dead by an organised crime gang in Dublin. Guerin's murder was a symptom of an unprecedented level of violent non-political crime in the Republic that has continued to breed dangerous gangs and, in some cases, has involved members of paramilitary organisations. It was unknown for journalists to be seriously assaulted in Ireland, but Guerin was not the last. On 28 September 2001 Martin O'Hagan of the *Sunday World* was targeted and gunned down in Northern Ireland by 'loyalist' (unionist) paramilitaries. On 18 April 2019 journalist Lyra McKee died in Derry, hit by reckless gunfire aimed at the Northern Ireland police by the splinter 'Real IRA'.

Economic progress in the Republic brought other problems too. The awarding of the Republic's first mobile licence in 1996 is controversial to this day, with the winner Denis O'Brien becoming one of Ireland's wealthiest businessmen. Both he and the relevant Fine Gael government minister then, Michael Lowry, have rejected any suggestion of wrong-doing.

In February 1997 *Dáil Éireann* set up a tribunal under Judge Brian McCracken to enquire urgently into payments in cash or in kind made directly or indirectly by Dunnes Stores (and/or Ben Dunne) to members of the Irish parliament between 1986 and 1996, and to their relatives and political parties. The trigger for this inquiry was revelations about gifts to Charles Haughey as *taoiseach* and to Michael Lowry as a government minister. The McCracken Tribunal unearthed no evidence of actual favours done by politicians in return for donations, but it rejected a substantial part of Charles Haughey's sworn evidence. It found that financial gifts to him were hidden from the Revenue Commissioners in offshore accounts. It also determined that the former Fine Gael minister Michael Lowry had evaded tax on contributions from Dunnes Stores. However, the tribunal found that a number of payments made by Ben Dunne personally to various other politicians were 'normal political contributions ... made on the basis of his personal regard for the individuals'. These included payments of between £2,500 and £5,000 each made to seven Fine Gael deputies including sometime *taoiseach* John Bruton. Dunne also contributed £15,000 to the successful presidential campaign of Mary Robinson, nominated by the Labour Party.

Speaking in *Dáil Éireann* on 10 September 1997 *Taoiseach* Bertie Ahern said it was 'unacceptable that in a manner hitherto concealed from the public a *taoiseach* [Haughey] should be personally supported to the tune of £1.3 million. It is appalling that any businessman should be able to believe, even if wrongly, that he could in any sense "buy" the *taoiseach*, or that he might have him in his pocket, if he ever needed him. By accepting such favours, Mr. Haughey thereby laid himself open to the possibility...' In the case of Michael Lowry, who received several hundred thousand pounds in cash or kind, the tribunal found he 'made himself vulnerable to all kinds of pressures from Dunne's Stores, had they chosen to apply those pressures', and that he was open to blackmail by others.

A further tribunal into payments, chaired by Judge Michael Moriarty, reported in 2011 that (Paragraph 60.39), 'payments and other benefits... were furnished by and on behalf of Mr Denis O'Brien to Mr Michael Lowry, and that these were demonstrably referable to the acts and conduct of Mr Lowry in regard to the GSM process [awarding the mobile phone licence in 1996], that inured [operated] to the benefit of Mr. O'Brien's winning consortium, Esat Digifone...' Moriarty also found

(60.44) that, 'between the granting of the second GSM licence to Esat Digifone in May 1996, and the transmission of Stg.£420,000.00 to complete the purchase of the latter of Mr. Lowry's English properties in December, 1999, Mr. O'Brien had made or facilitated payments to Mr. Lowry of £147,000.00, [and] Stg.£300,000.00 and a benefit equivalent to a payment in the form of Mr. O'Brien's support for a loan of Stg. £420,000.00.' Lowry has continued to be elected by his loyal constituents in Co. Tipperary. He and Denis O'Brien deny wrongdoing and contest tribunal findings. Many citizens suspect that the problem of certain payments to politicians in planning and other matters is greater than has been publicly demonstrated.

On 6 June 1997 Fianna Fáil returned to power in the Republic. Its leader Bertie Ahern formed a government with the small right-of-centre Progressive Democrats party. Remaining as *taoiseach* until 2008, Ahern was to become closely associated with the Northern Ireland Peace Process and the Belfast/Good Friday Agreement, and also with the most golden years of prosperity known as the 'Celtic Tiger'. He would finally crash to earth politically amid a series of scandals that colour his comments of September 1997 quoted above about Haughey accepting financial favours.

In November 1997 Mary McAleese, a barrister and broadcaster, became the eight president of Ireland – and second woman in that office. Although nominated by the right-of-centre Fianna Fáil party, McAleese was seen as being independent-minded. Born in Northern Ireland, her bridge-building efforts as president included celebrating at her official residence in Dublin's Phoenix Park the great Northern Ireland Unionist holiday of the Twelfth of July. This marks the victory of the Protestant

William of Orange over the Catholic King James at the Battle of the Boyne in Ireland in 1690. McAleese, also a civil and canon lawyer, has challenged conservative authorities of the Catholic Church to which she belongs, including on homosexuality and misogyny. While president, she defied her Church's rules on one occasion by taking communion at a Protestant cathedral in Dublin. The fact that condemnation of this by an Irish cardinal had little or no adverse impact on the public's opinion of her was an indication of the alienation of Irish Catholics from their institutional Church. McAleese served a second term from 2004.

On 10 April 1998 the momentous Belfast Agreement was signed by Ireland and the UK. It was the culmination of an ongoing peace process in Northern Ireland that saw the main paramilitary organisations lay down their arms ('decommission') and commit themselves to supporting constitutional politics. The remarkable Mo Mowlam, UK Secretary of State for Northern Ireland, played a central role in bringing it about, as did Prime Minister Tony Blair and *Taoiseach* Bertie Ahern. The Belfast Agreement is frequently called the 'Good Friday Agreement' because it was signed on the Friday before Easter on which Christians each year commemorate the crucifixion of Jesus. The agreement affirms that if a majority in each part of Ireland wishes to unite in an independent all-island state then the UK government will not oppose or stop Northern Ireland leaving the United Kingdom.

The Belfast/Good Friday Agreement created a framework for the two Northern Ireland traditions to share power. This included the Assembly, with its executive composed of representatives of parties from across the old nationalist/unionist divide; a Ministerial Council to develop north-south co-operation between both parts of Ireland; and a British-Irish

Council to promote east-west relationships between Ireland and Britain. These institutions have worked only intermittently in the years since the Belfast/Good Friday Agreement, and the Irish and British governments continue to negotiate with the Northern Ireland parties to build trust.

Mo Mowlam (centre), UK Secretary of State for Northern Ireland, with Liz O'Donnell, the Republic's Minister of State for Foreign Affairs, at Glencree Centre for Reconciliation, Co. Wicklow, February 1998. *Courtesy Glencree Centre.*

The peace process, including the Belfast/Good Friday Agreement, ultimately led to the decommissioning of weapons by paramilitaries on each 'side' and the ending of the levels of violence that had plagued Northern Ireland during the previous decades. With both the Republic of Ireland and the UK already members of the European Union, committed to a single market, this meant that the Irish border was almost invisible once security checks were removed. Speed limit signs became the residual indication of a change of jurisdiction, being in miles on the northern side and kilometres on the southern side of the border.

Referendums on the Belfast/Good Friday Agreement were held north and south of the Irish border on 22 May 1998. In the North, 71% approved of it and in the South 94%.

On 25 June 1998, in the first elections to the newly established power-sharing Northern Ireland Assembly, the moderate and nationalist Social Democratic and Labour Party (SDLP) did well. It won the highest share of votes (21.97%). The Ulster Unionist Party (UUP), fared worse than expected, with a 21.25% share. However, when all votes were eventually allocated under the system of proportional representation, these percentages translated into 28 seats for the UUP and just 24 for the SDLP. It meant that the long-dominant UUP had still won an assembly majority and was therefore entitled to nominate the assembly's first minister. Its leader David Trimble was subsequently appointed to that position, while Séamus Mallon of the SDLP became deputy first minister. For now the relative moderates of Northern Ireland's politics held the middle ground under the Belfast/Good Friday Agreement. Few foresaw how quickly this would change.

At times in the years that followed, when sufficient cross-party agreement was absent to sustain power-sharing, the Assembly was suspended by the UK government. Northern Ireland was then administered directly by the UK government in accordance with the terms of the Belfast/Good Friday Agreement. The extent to which suspension has been necessary means that the agreement has not worked as well in practice as had been hoped.

There was another terrible bombing in Northern Ireland on 15 August 1998. Twenty-nine people died and more than two hundred were injured at Omagh, Co. Tyrone. The 'Real IRA', a splinter group from the IRA, carried it out. The bombers had telephoned wholly inadequate warnings. The outrage made people north and south more determined than ever to see the peace process work. Intelligence agencies had received vital information about the planned bombing, but to protect their sources did not share this in time with the police.

In October 1998 the Nobel Peace Prize was awarded to John Hume and David Trimble for their efforts to find a peaceful solution to the conflict in Northern Ireland. During the previous thirty years, the conflict had cost more than 3,500 lives. The Nobel committee stated: 'John Hume [of the SDLP] has throughout been the clearest and most consistent of Northern Ireland's political leaders in his work for a peaceful solution.' It added that 'As the leader of the traditionally predominant party in Northern Ireland, David Trimble [of the Ulster Unionist Party] showed great political courage when, at a critical stage of the process, he advocated solutions which led to the peace agreement.'

On 1 January 1999, the Republic of Ireland became one of the eleven founding members of the European Monetary Union. The United Kingdom did not. Ireland adopted the euro. The distinctive coins of the independent Irish state, finely designed and adopted in 1928 and featuring a range of animals as decided by a committee chaired by the poet William Butler Yeats, were completely replaced by euro coins in 2002.

During the 1990s the international Dublin Literary Award was established. Originally sponsored by the IMPAC company, this annual event is now entirely organised and funded by Dublin City Council. The prize of €100,000 is generous, as if Ireland wishes to make up somehow for decades of narrow censorship of books and films in the mid-twentieth century. The first winner of the prize was David Malouf, in 1996, for his novel *Remembering Babylon*. Other winners have included Tahar Ben Jelloun for *This Blinding Absence of Light* in 2004 and Alice Zeniter for the *Art of Losing* in 2022. Irish winners have included Colm Tóibín (*The Master*), Kevin Barry (*City of Bohane*), Colum McCann (*Let the Great World Spin*) and Anna Burns (whose *Milkman* also won the Booker Prize in 2018). When the winning book is a translation into English, the translator gets one quarter of the prize money. The evolution of a publicly tolerant attitude towards authors in the Republic was no doubt bitter-sweet for Irish writers such as Edna O'Brien and John McGahern who had spent years writing in the face of disapproval and censorship. Their first books, including *The Country Girls* and *The Dark*, were banned in the 1960s. It is droll how in the public mind, between 1970 and 2020, James Joyce and Samuel Beckett went from being regarded as experimental intellectuals on the margins of Irish society to being proudly elevated symbols of cultural achievement and openness. University College Dublin even renamed its main library after Joyce, while images of the two men – along with that of the once discomforting Oscar Wilde – have sprouted up around the city in pubs and on tourist trails. Today, the Irish Naval Service even includes patrol vessels called the Samuel Beckett and James Joyce, alongside the William Butler Yeats!

Boom and Bust: 2000-2009

It was a disaster waiting to happen. Between 2002 and the end of 2007, lending by the six main banks in the Republic to the construction and property sectors grew at an annual rate more than six times that of the Irish economy. The total amount of lending for speculative construction and property projects increased from about €4bn to about €35bn in the same period. The banks funded such loans by incurring foreign debts. Their lending growth rates far exceeded those in the UK and other EU countries. In 2008 a global crisis was triggered by the collapse of Lehman Brothers and other financial institutions in the United States. By then, the Republic of Ireland was especially vulnerable.

Economic growth in the Republic in the last quarter of the twentieth century had been fueled by both EU membership and inward US investment in Ireland. It bred over-confidence and even arrogance about the future of an island that for centuries had long known great poverty.

The social democratic traditions of many European countries fostered a level of EU economic regulation that was not only inconvenient at times for American capitalists investing large sums in the Republic (using Ireland to build their commercial base within the EU) but also frustrating for native speculators trying to get richer quickly. Cultural and ideological tensions were identified in a key speech by *Tánaiste* Mary Harney, leader of the small but then influential neo-liberal Progressive Democrats. Addressing the American Bar Association in Dublin on 21 July 2000, she remarked that,

> History and geography have placed Ireland in a very special position between America and Europe. History has bound this country very

closely to the United States. Down the centuries millions of Irish people crossed the Atlantic in search of a new life in a new world. And that tradition of emigration laid the foundation for the strong social, economic and political ties between our two countries today. Geography has placed this country on the edge of the European continent. One of our most significant achievements as an independent nation was our entry, almost thirty years ago, into what is now the European Union. Today, we have strong social, economic and political ties with the EU.

Given that there were such 'strong ties', the Republic now took the EU by surprise. Under the Irish constitution, Irish citizens must approve international treaties by referendum before they are ratified. A referendum to approve the EU Treaty of Nice was held on 7 June 2001. The main purpose of that treaty was to make the institutions that governed the EU more efficient and responsive in the context of its growing membership. The treaty also dealt with issues such as common foreign and security policy. Previous referendums had approved membership of the EEC itself (1972), the Single European Act (1987), the treaty on European Union (the Maastricht Treaty, 1992) and the Treaty of Amsterdam (1998). The 'yes' results then had reflected the Republic's loyalty to the EU ideal. Now, suddenly, the Nice proposal was rejected. Had other EU countries, including the UK, been required to hold similar referendums might their citizens have likewise rejected the treaty? How might people in Northern Ireland have voted? If the Irish were now sending a signal to the EU not to take them for granted, leading Irish politicians were alarmed because the need for all member states to ratify the treaty meant that – in the absence of popular votes elsewhere – Ireland appeared to be exceptionally obstructive. Steps would be taken quickly to persuade the electorate to change its mind.

Meanwhile, in Northern Ireland, the 2001 UK general election proved significant because the result reflected a political polarisation that, paradoxically, emerged after the Belfast/Good Friday Agreement of 1998. With the IRA now ostensibly committed to peace, perhaps nationalists felt freer to vote for Sinn Féin. For the first time throughout the province that party won more support than the Social Democratic and Labour Party (SDLP). The difference between their votes was small but significant, signalling a rise in the fortunes of the more militantly republican party that was to grow as support for the SDLP shrank. This was despite the fact that although Sinn Féin now takes seats to which it is elected throughout Ireland, it still refuses as a matter of principle to sit in the UK parliament at Westminster when it wins seats there. On the unionist side in 2001 the moderate Ulster Unionist Party was still outperforming Ian Paisley's DUP, but that too was going to change.

In November 2001 the old Royal Ulster Constabulary was subsumed into the new Police Service of Northern Ireland (PSNI), a branding and organisational change intended in part to signify a more inclusive approach to policing in Northern Ireland. However, progress towards reconciliation again slowed during 2002. It was feared that the IRA was not fully committed to peace. The UK government had to suspend the first Northern Ireland Assembly when unionist parties withdrew following a police raid on Sinn Féin's offices. The raid was based on allegations that Sinn Féin staff members were gathering intelligence for the IRA. The assembly was to remain suspended until 2007, despite the fact that elections to it were held in 2003. Whenever the assembly is suspended, the province is ruled directly by the UK government in London – which displeases nationalists especially.

South of the border in December 2001, the fact that Ireland (so long witness to the emigration of its own people) was now itself a destination for desperate migrants became shockingly clear. Along with furniture coming from Milan, the bodies of eight people from outside the EU were found in a truck. During the next twenty years the number of people seeking refuge in Ireland was to soar.

As Ireland changed, conservatives resisted further liberalisation. In 2002 they persuaded Bertie Ahern's government to hold another constitutional referendum to tighten up the state's already tight controls on abortion. Again, as in 1992, it was proposed that evidence that a woman was suicidal due to her pregnancy should not be a ground for an abortion. A danger to life was the sole exception to the Republic's existing ban on abortion. Ahern's government even proposed stiffer prison terms for those performing an illegal abortion. The proposals generated much public debate but were narrowly defeated.

The Irish electorate had made a point when rejecting the EU Treaty of Nice during 2001. It is not entirely clear what that point was, as there never has been the same level of animosity in Ireland towards the EU as that found in Britain – whether expressed there through parliament, the tabloid press or ultimately the Brexit referendum. Irish people had strong historic links with France and Spain during centuries of British occupation. Moreover, the Republic's membership of the EU had facilitated social and economic reforms. Citizens learnt to embrace it as a maturing or even liberating reality. Many who originally saw membership as an infringement of economic and political sovereignty were happily reconciled with it and found that their fears were exaggerated. The agricultural sector benefited greatly and industry overall grew. Citizens felt freed from an historic over-dependence on trade with Britain and were proud to be seen as 'good Europeans'. So, having indicated in the first referendum on the Treaty of Nice that they would not be taken for granted, the people of the Republic in October 2002 accepted a fresh proposal from the Irish government that came with vague reassurances. This time they voted in favour of the Nice Treaty. There were sighs of relief. However, the electorate appears to have enjoyed its power to shock and, on the eve of the economic crash of 2008, it was to repeat its performance when it came to the Lisbon Treaty.

The second set of elections to the new power-sharing Northern Ireland Assembly took place in November 2003. Reverend Ian Paisley's Democratic Unionist Party surpassed the more moderate Ulster Unionist Party (UUP) to become the largest unionist party in the assembly. The UUP had dominated politics in Northern Ireland since the 1920s, but no longer. A perception even among some UUP members that too many concessions were being made to nationalists helped the DUP. Notably at this election Sinn Féin also increased its lead over the SDLP and came second of all parties in Northern Ireland. The more moderate unionist and nationalist parties were being pushed aside and would remain in the wings, while the more polarised parties faced the challenge of governing together if power-sharing was to work. The response to that challenge did not result in an executive being formed immediately. The assembly remained suspended.

On 29 March 2004 the Republic of Ireland became the first country internationally to introduce a comprehensive ban on smoking in public places. The ease with which the ban was accepted by the public, including in pubs, surprised many. In December 2004 George W. Bush became the latest US president to visit Ireland, in his case coming for a few hours to Dromoland Castle in Co. Clare near Shannon Airport, for a summit with European Union leaders. He was met by protests against the war in Iraq. Protesters managed to block a main route to the castle, and the White House Press Corps in their special coaches had to make a laborious detour along rural back roads. The present author was also on one of those coaches, and was struck by the extent to which the visitors commented in surprise on the good quality and modernity of houses along the way. Perhaps they expected dirt roads and old thatched cottages.

December 2004 also witnessed one of the biggest robberies in history, when a gang escaped with over £26m from the Northern Bank in Belfast. It is believed that senior Sinn Féin members had sanctioned the robbery and that those who carried it out were members of the IRA. A decade later the *Belfast Telegraph* recalled the raid as 'a huge setback to efforts to rebuild a fragile peace process'. While a Co. Cork financial adviser was convicted of laundering £3m from the haul, the vast bulk of the money was never recovered and may have been used to finance Sinn Féin's political progress. Another blow to the peace process came a month after the Northern Bank robbery when members of the IRA murdered Robert McCartney, following an incident in a pub, and subsequently intimidated witnesses. The IRA had clearly not gone away, despite the Belfast/Good Friday Agreement.

Yet, because of the peace process generally, public attitudes were mellowing. In April 2005 in an historic amendment to its rules, the all-Ireland Gaelic Athletic Association (GAA) agreed to allow soccer and rugby teams to play fixtures at its headquarter ground at Croke Park in Dublin. Those teams' usual international venue on Lansdowne Road was then being redeveloped into a new stadium (currently named 'the Aviva'). The GAA had been established as a nationalist sporting movement, with its members playing a distinct form of 'Gaelic football' as well as the stick sports of hurling and camogie. The 2005 decision was historic because for the previous century members of the GAA had identified soccer and rugby as 'garrison games' associated with the British presence in Ireland. Indeed, until 1971 another GAA rule had provided that 'Any member of the Association who plays or encourages in any way rugby, football [soccer], hockey or any imported game which is calculated to injuriously affect our National Pastimes' was to be suspended. This ban had extended even to members of the association caught attending such other sports, including in 1938 the President of Ireland Douglas Hyde – who was a Protestant. The GAA is deeply rooted in Irish life north and south of the border, especially in rural areas. It supports a range of community activities. Its sportsmen are amateurs, not professionals. The rules against members participating in other sports had stood in the way of better relations on the island, and made little sense to many people who enjoyed watching and even playing soccer and rugby as well as Gaelic games. Its more recent inclusive approach has seen it embracing immigrants from cultures overseas.

As mentioned already, since 1920 rugby has continued to be organised on an all-Ireland basis but there are separate international soccer teams for Northern Ireland and the Republic. Recognising the nature of its structure, the Irish Rugby Football Union now uses two anthems, one being the national anthem of the Republic ('Amhrán na bhFiann') – which has strong republican connotations – and the other 'Ireland's Call' – specially composed by Phil Coulter from Derry in Northern Ireland and first heard at the 1995 Rugby World Cup in South Africa. In partnership with Bill Martin, Coulter had previously written popular hits. While 'Ireland's Call' is bland, its chorus optimistically declares 'Ireland, Ireland, Together standing tall; Shoulder to shoulder, We'll answer Ireland's call.' Both anthems are sung and played at fixtures in Dublin, but only 'Ireland's Call' abroad. At rugby and soccer internationals, Irish supporters have also adopted an unofficial and sentimental anthem – 'The Fields of Athenry'. What might be the anthem of a united Ireland is anyone's guess.

A billboard campaign by the Gaelic Athletic Association welcomes diversity in sport, 2020. The poster is overlaid lightly with the names of hundreds of GAA clubs. Photographer Eoin Holland. *Courtesy GAA.*

During this first decade of the twenty-first century the Irish Book Awards were initiated, a marker along with the Dublin Literary Award of the continuing popularity of reading in Ireland. Its winners are something of a 'who's who' of popular Irish authors and have included writers of novels such as Joseph O'Connor, Bernard MacLaverty, Anne Enright, Sebastian Barry, John Banville, Roddy Doyle, Patrick McCabe, Sally Rooney, Donal Ryan and Louise Kennedy.

With Sinn Féin determined to increase its democratic political mandate on both sides of the border, in light of the Belfast/Good Friday Agreement, any continuing activity by members of the paramilitary IRA wing was counterproductive for it. On 28 July 2005 the IRA formally stated that it had ordered an end to its armed campaign and instructed its units to 'dump arms'. Within months the Independent International Commission on Decommissioning (IICD), a body approved by both the Irish and UK governments, satisfied itself that the IRA had in fact completed its decommissioning of arms. This confirmation opened the way to further political progress.

During 2006 a vital supplementary deal was struck at St Andrews in Scotland. It tied up loose ends of the Belfast/Good Friday Agreement and saw power-sharing restored in practice in Belfast after a gap of five years. The third Northern Ireland Assembly, elected on 7 March 2007, was remarkable not least for the cordial working relationship promptly established between First Minister Rev. Ian Paisley, the unionist firebrand, and Deputy First Minister Martin McGuinness, the former IRA commander. Media nicknamed them 'the Chuckle Brothers' (from a BBC children's show) because they were so amiable and smiled so much when in public. The DUP and Sinn Féin were consolidating their dominance over politics in Northern Ireland, at the expense of more moderate parties.

McGuinness had been Sinn Féin's chief negotiator in the Northern Ireland peace process that led to the Belfast/Good Friday Agreement and he was to continue to serve as deputy first minister until 2017 – while the first ministers during that period were successively Ian Paisley, Peter Robinson and Arlene Foster, all of the DUP. Paisley, who had denounced the Pope as the antichrist and who was once the very epitome of Ulster unionist intransigence, actually found himself pushed aside. On BBC Northern Ireland in January 2014 he said that senior figures in the DUP persuaded him to resign as first minister in 2008, after a canvass found that many DUP members of the assembly were unhappy with his 'chuckling' appearances alongside McGuinness.

There were political changes of a different kind in the Republic. The Green Party entered government there for the first time in 2007, as a very small member of a coalition formed largely by Bertie Ahern's Fianna Fáil with the centre-right but shrinking Progressive Democrats. In the general election on 24 May 2007 the Greens won six seats, the PDs two. On 6 May 2008 Ahern himself stepped down as *taoiseach* and leader of the mainstream Fianna Fáil party, and was replaced by his minister for finance Brian Cowen. The *Irish Independent* described Ahern's 'surprise' announcement as 'sensational'. It came following contradictions in evidence that Ahern gave to a tribunal of enquiry into planning matters (the Mahon tribunal), concerning certain bank deposits in sterling lodged into his accounts. In its final report, this tribunal would later find, among other things, that 'Much of the explanation provided by Mr Ahern as to the source of the substantial funds identified and inquired into in the course of the Tribunal's public hearings was deemed by the Tribunal to have been untrue.' It was satisfied that Ahern had not given 'a truthful account' as to the source of certain monies lodged to his benefit. It 'rejected the various explanations proffered by Mr Ahern as to how he came into possession' of certain monies (Mahon Tribunal Report, paragraphs 12.04, 12.09, 13.01).

It was also in 2008 that the Republic's electorate again showed the EU that it was not to be taken for granted. A referendum was held in June on a proposal to ratify the Lisbon Treaty. This treaty proposed to amend, but not replace, the two main treaties that governed the EU. Its somewhat technical proposal was defeated. Irish voters had been persuaded to reverse their earlier obstructive decision of 2001 to reject the Treaty of Nice. This time they were again to recant, not least due to the shock of the economic crash that came soon afterwards in 2008. Voters endorsed the Lisbon Treaty when it was dressed up with reassurances and put to them once more on 2 October 2009.

The international financial crash of 2008 came to a head in Ireland, traumatically, on the night of 29 September 2008. Irish financial institutions faced bankruptcy and the government was stampeded into guaranteeing their liquidity and stability. It was later claimed that *Taoiseach* Brian Cowen and Minister for Finance Brian Lenihan had no real choice in the matter – that they could not afford to gamble on anything less than the state taking on the bulk of the banks' liabilities. During the night other members of the Irish cabinet were phoned to give their consent to the deal. One said, 'They wanted my assent and it was put to me that this was absolutely essential or the whole financial system would topple in the morning' (*Irish Independent*, 30 Sept. 2018). Lenihan was to justify the decision that night by saying later 'The wellbeing of our nation and our people was under threat. The State Guarantee introduced overnight on the 29th of September 2008 pulled us back from the brink' (*Dáil Éireann Debates*, 16 Sept. 2019).

The Irish banks had recklessly lent money to big borrowers, ostensibly on the basis of property assets, but the value of those assets had dropped dramatically and, in some cases, was never what it had seemed. The government responded now by effectively taking about €400 billion of taxpayers' money (a very large sum for a small country such as Ireland) and using it to fill holes in the banks' vaults. Despite a number of public investigations into what had happened, there was never a full and comprehensive account of where the money originally lent by banks and now replaced by the state ended up. The cry 'we were all at it' was heard from those who were willing to minimise what had happened by spreading the blame, as though young couples who took easy loans pushed at them by avaricious financial institutions were in the same league as speculators and others to whom the banks gave massive advances to invest not only in Ireland but overseas. There had indeed been what a governor of the Central Bank of Ireland would in 2010 describe as 'a world-beating property bubble', but it was not caused by ordinary citizens who were now saddled with large personal loans or mortgages in a shrinking economy and where their homes were worth far less than what they owed on them. The governor stated that the lending debacle was 'driven by an over-optimistic misinterpretation of the nature of the Celtic Tiger and the basis of the earlier success' of Ireland's economy in the immediately preceding years.

Financial matters went from bad to worse in the Republic. In November 2008 the Department of Finance was advised that Anglo-Irish Bank's total commercial real estate lending constituted more than 80% of its total loans, which was more than twice the equivalent for Allied Irish Bank (AIB) and the Bank of Ireland, Ireland's two main banks. There were serious deficiencies in Anglo-Irish Bank's annual reports. Subsequent revelations about the manner in which the relatively new Anglo-Irish Bank was administered before it was finally taken into public ownership scandalised the Irish public. The bank came to represent in the public mind what had gone wrong with Ireland in its 'Celtic Tiger' phase, including inadequate regulation and the indulgence of greed at the expense of the public. The prosecution of the bank's former chairman and chief executive 'Seánie' Fitzpatrick, for misleading the bank's auditors and other alleged criminal offences, resulted in his acquittal. A judge criticised the Office of the Director of Corporate Enforcement. This contributed to a public perception of broader inadequacies in how the Irish state deals with alleged wrongdoing by elites.

On 15 January 2009 the government of the Republic announced that it would take Anglo-Irish Bank into public ownership. This added to the burden on taxpayers, already stuck with banking liabilities running to many billions. The impact of the bank guarantee on the state's finances was considerable, contributing as it did to a recession that lasted for years and limiting public expenditure in other areas. Later in 2009 the Irish government established the controversial National Asset Management Agency (NAMA). Its function was to take over substantial property-related debts from the banks and to get the best possible return from them in the unfavourable circumstances of the time. While NAMA appears generally to have functioned efficiently in respect to its statutory objectives, some critics believe that it might have done much more to promote the construction and sale of affordable housing and thus helped to prevent the severe shortage of available new homes relative to demand in Ireland today. There is public anger that, since the crash, international 'vulture funds' seem to enjoy preferential treatment over individuals and couples when it comes to the acquisition of residential properties. The sale of NAMA's £4.5 billion Northern Ireland portfolio has also generated controversy, following claims that £7m lodged in an Isle of Man bank account was intended for a Northern Ireland politician who was part of the deal. Those claims are denied.

Meanwhile in Northern Ireland, as politicians to varying extents tried to make power-sharing work as a form of government, small groups of violent dissidents continued to kill people. On 7 March 2009, for example, dissident nationalist paramilitaries shot dead two British soldiers near Antrim. No British troops had been murdered in Northern Ireland since 1997. Two days later Constable Stephen Carroll was killed in Co. Down, the first policeman shot dead in Northern Ireland since 1997. It was clear that neither political progress in Northern Ireland nor economic progress in the Republic could be taken for granted.

Recovery: 2010-2020

In a speech in Tokyo on 19 August 2010, the governor of the Central Bank of Ireland Patrick Honohan claimed that the Republic of Ireland was 'now the most globalised economy on earth'. He noted that by the year 2007 'the Celtic Tiger, it seemed, could grow as quickly as its Asian cousins and for a sustained period'. Given that the economy of the Republic had crashed in 2008, he conceded 'It is natural for observers to ask: was it all a chimera: a bubble masquerading as a tiger?' He stressed that Ireland was now giving a lead to other countries by way of its recovery.

Not everyone in Ireland in 2010 felt as buoyant as he did, with the economic impact of the crash continuing to hit many individuals, families and companies for years. Popular sentiment was reflected in a sharp retrospective by the economist Jim Power some years later when he wrote that 'Irish bankers created utterly ridiculous and ultimately disastrously unsustainable exposures to creditors …. Basically, the banking elite forgot all of the rules of prudent lending as they got caught up in a greed- and hubris-driven circus' (*Irish Examiner*, 10 Nov. 2021). People asked why so many economists had failed to foresee and warn of the disaster.

By the autumn of 2010 the loss of investor confidence in Ireland triggered a vicious cycle. Deposit outflows from the banking sector accelerated and the cost of government borrowing grew further. The Republic was obliged to agree to the 'Economic Adjustment Programme for Ireland' – commonly known as 'the bail-out'. This was an agreement for billions in financial assistance to which the EU, the European Central Bank and the International Monetary Fund were parties. Ireland came under great pressure to enter the programme quickly, not least because it was feared internationally that the Irish situation might have a contagious impact elsewhere in Europe. The bailout severely restricted the economic autonomy of the Irish state – if not its sovereignty – for three years. That some of the package came by way of bilateral loans from three specific EU countries which included the United Kingdom was particularly galling for many Irish citizens. Irish people saw the bailout as a humiliation, but a necessary one. Citizens were relieved when the Republic's economy recovered quickly enough to exit the programme in 2013 and the state did not have to renew it. Reuters reported then that 'Three years after going cap in hand to international lenders to avert bankruptcy, Ireland has officially ended its bailout in a landmark for the eurozone's efforts to resolve its debt crisis' (*Telegraph* [UK], 14 Dec. 2013). The Republic's financial indiscipline in creating a crisis was largely forgiven abroad due to its discipline in dealing with the consequences.

In the general election of February 2011 the voters of the Republic had a chance to respond politically to the crash of 2008 and its aftermath, and for which they now held the once mighty Fianna Fáil party responsible. Fianna Fáil had a disastrous result, cut to just twenty seats against its main rival Fine Gael which won seventy-six, while the Labour Party had its best ever outcome winning thirty-seven. The Greens lost their six seats. Fine Gael's Enda Kenny became *taoiseach*, while Joan Burton – the first woman to lead the Labour Party – was made *tánaiste* (deputy prime minister). This result might have led entirely to the demise of Fianna Fáil had not the new coalition of Fine Gael and Labour been so lacklustre, albeit while struggling under a heavy burden of inherited economic woes.

The arrival of Queen Elizabeth II in Dublin in May 2011 brought some light relief for the Irish public. Queen Elizabeth's was the first such trip by any British monarch since the foundation of the independent Irish state. During her long reign she made more than two dozen carefully guarded visits to Northern Ireland. But none of them was more symbolically important than her only visit to the Republic. She opened her speech at a state dinner in Dublin Castle with five words in Irish, and laid a wreath at the city's memorial to those who died fighting British imperialism in Ireland. She herself had known personally Lord Louis Mountbatten, who was her cousin and her husband's uncle, murdered by the IRA in 1979 during a private visit to his favourite destination in the Republic. Her 2011 visit was not her first or last gesture of reconciliation. One year later, as the Church of Ireland website was to recall in a 2022 press release, 'Her Majesty demonstrated the power a simple handshake can play in reconciliation when she and former IRA commander, the late Martin McGuinness, exchanged just such a handshake at a charity event in Belfast' (ireland.anglican.org).

A few days after Queen Elizabeth left the republic, Barack Obama became the latest US president to visit Ireland. On a very brief trip, he went to the village of Moneygall where descendants of his Irish ancestor lived. Later, a motorway stop on the Dublin to Limerick road nearby was named Barack Obama Plaza. His speech to a large crowd in Dublin included a joke referencing the prefix letter 'O' with its apostrophe common before Irish family names: 'Hello, Ireland! (Applause). My name is Barack Obama (Applause). Of the Moneygall Obamas (Applause). And I've come home to find the apostrophe that we lost somewhere along the way (Laughter and applause).' Obama recalled the visit to Ireland of the black activist Frederick Douglass (1818–95), 'an escaped slave and our great abolitionist', and his 'unlikely friendship' with Daniel O'Connell, Ireland's most famous nationalist politician of the nineteenth century: 'His time here, Frederick Douglass said, defined him not as a color but as a man. And it strengthened the non-violent campaign he would return home to wage.'

In November 2011 Michael D. Higgins was inaugurated as President of Ireland. He was to be re-elected in 2018. A former coalition government minister of the minority Labour Party, O'Higgins is a poet and radical intellectual of humble social background. He is also a former president of Galway United Football Club. He was the third successive elected president who stood somewhat apart from the mainstream political establishment. Voters were increasingly opting for independent-minded candidates to represent Ireland in the largely ceremonial role of president.

During 2012 Katie Taylor of Bray, Co. Wicklow, won a gold medal for Ireland in the lightweight category at the Olympic Games in London – the first time that the Olympics included women's boxing. Taylor came to be seen as Ireland's leading sportsperson for a while. In 1992 at Barcelona Michael Carruth had won Ireland's only other Olympic gold medal for boxing. Taylor's was the first Irish Olympic Gold of any kind since Michelle Smith took three golds and a bronze for swimming at Atlanta in 1996. Smith's double triumph as the first woman to win a medal for Ireland and as the most successful Olympian of any gender for Ireland was later overshadowed by her ban for tampering with urine samples. She became a barrister in Dublin. After Taylor, the next members of an Irish team to win Olympic gold were Kellie Harrington in the lightweight boxing division and both Fintan McCarthy and Paul O'Donovan in the lightweight double sculls event – all at Tokyo in 2021.

On 28 October 2012 Savita Halappanavar, a pregnant woman aged 31, died of sepsis at University Hospital Galway. She had asked for an abortion several times but was refused. Her family believed that, due to her particular medical circumstances, she would have survived had her wish been granted. The case reignited debate about Ireland's very restrictive abortion law. More general concerns about the way that the Irish state had long treated women and children were partly addressed by a referendum passed in November 2012 that explicitly acknowledged that children have rights, and that the State is obliged 'as far as practicable' by its laws to protect and vindicate those rights.

Efforts by the Irish government to reform political institutions were stumbling, and the public rejected referendum proposals to give parliamentary committees greater power and to abolish completely the senate. The particular proposals created public distrust by failing to persuade voters that the changes as drafted would improve the political sphere.

Continuing public revelations heightened public concern about the past abuse and mistreatment of children in the Republic. In one response *Dáil Éireann*, the Irish parliament, acknowledged 'the need to establish the facts regarding the deaths of almost 800 children at the Bon Secours Sisters institution in Tuam, Co. Galway between 1925 and 1961', and also regarding arrangements for the burial of those children. It also acknowledged a need to examine similar institutions elsewhere in the State historically. The deaths of children at Tuam had been brought to light by the sustained efforts of a local woman, Catherine Corless, who discovered that at least some of the dead babies were buried in an underground water tank. In 2015 the government established the Commission of Investigation into Mother and Baby Homes. Its report five years later (available online) included the commission's observation that 'Ireland appears to be the only country where large numbers of unmarried pregnant women left their native country'. It found a high level of mortality among babies deposited in the institutions.

Irish people have also been appalled to learn of another scandal involving irregular adoption practices at some such baby 'homes' and elsewhere, and not only at Catholic institutions. The extent to which the public at large once shared harsh attitudes to unmarried mothers and their children, and tolerated inadequate arrangements to care for them, is a continuing matter of discussion.

A significant change in Ireland's laws on personal freedom came in May 2015. By a majority of two to one in a referendum, the Republic's voters approved a constitutional amendment to provide that 'Marriage may be contracted in accordance with law by two persons without distinction as to their sex'. Such a national referendum on marital equality, recognising the status of same-sex couples, was unique.

Lesbian and Gay Pride Day, Dublin 2003. In 2015 the Republic of Ireland became the first country whose voters endorsed same-sex marriage in a referendum. Photograph Christopher Robson. *Courtesy National Library of Ireland.*

Same-sex marriages had been allowed by statute law in Britain since 2014, although that law did not extend to Northern Ireland and was not underpinned by the force of a referendum result. Same-sex marriage proposals were blocked in the Northern Ireland Assembly by the

Democratic Unionist Party. On 13 January 2020 such marriages finally became possible there when the UK government authorised them, despite the Northern Ireland Assembly's failure to do so.

Efforts to sustain a power-sharing devolved government in Northern Ireland continued to be problematic. During 2016 an executive was formed again by the two major parties, the Democratic Unionist Party and Sinn Féin. DUP leader Arlene Foster became the first woman premier in Ireland when appointed first minister of the Northern Ireland Assembly to succeed Peter Robinson. No woman has ever been *taoiseach* of the Republic. As a child Foster saw her father John Kelly, a farmer and reserve policeman, crawl through the front door of their home after the IRA shot him.

The Republic's general election of February 2016 was a vote of no confidence in the main political parties, with the electorate growing increasingly dissatisfied with economic and social developments since the crash of 2008. While Fine Gael returned to government under *Taoiseach* Enda Kenny, it did so in a fragmented *Dáil Éireann* and with its own numbers considerably reduced. Sinn Féin, which unlike Fine Gael and Fianna Fáil is an all-island political party, was getting stronger both north and south. It became at this election the third largest party in *Dáil Éireann*.

On 23 June 2016 a fateful day for Ireland and Britain, just over half of those who voted in the United Kingdom (51.9%) opted to leave the European Union, although most voters in both Scotland and Northern Ireland opposed this option known as 'Brexit'. The majority against Brexit in Northern Ireland consisted of a majority of Catholics/nationalists together with a minority of Protestants/unionists. Complex negotiations between the UK and the EU followed the 2016 vote before the UK left the EU on 31 January 2020. At the centre of negotiations was Northern Ireland. The Republic insisted that the border in Ireland (also about to be a border between the EU and a newly non-EU United Kingdom) must not become a hard barrier undermining the UK's international treaty obligations under the Belfast/Good Friday Agreement on peace in Ireland.

Brexit makes frictionless trade between the EU and the UK impossible. However, the EU and UK also agreed a 'Northern Ireland Protocol' that created special controls that have allowed Northern Ireland to remain within the UK customs territory while, at the same time, having access to the EU Single Market. This facilitates all-Ireland co-operation in areas such as agriculture, transport, education and tourism, and ensures that the island's Single Electricity Market can be preserved.

As the Republic struggled to recover from the crash of 2008, it jealously guarded its right to give favourable tax rates to foreign companies coming to Ireland. In August 2016 the European Commission concluded that the Republic of Ireland had granted undue tax benefits of up to €13 billion to Apple. The benefits were considered illegal under EU state aid rules, with Apple having paid proportionately less tax than certain other competing or comparative businesses in Europe. Ireland was now expected to recover the illegal aid. Apple is one of the largest of a number of very large multinationals in the Republic, with other big corporate investors from abroad including Intel, Microsoft, Google and Pfizer. Indeed, Apple and Microsoft alone appear to have paid the state between them a total of €4 billion in corporate tax in 2020.

The overall financial success of Ireland's inward investment programme since the 1960s has greatly helped to fuel the state's growing prosperity in the past fifty years. But it also makes the state vulnerable, being so dependent on revenue from corporation tax that the shock of a sudden downturn in that sector could be traumatic. The ten biggest corporations are said to account for about half of the state's total corporate tax revenue. The extent to which Ireland's policies have lured in US companies has also been an issue in recent US presidential elections, when candidates promised to bring jobs 'home' to America. But such companies want an EU base. When Brexit made Britain less attractive in that context, Ireland became even more alluring. The Irish government strongly defends its tax incentives, arguing that other states have their own ways of being competitive. In October 2021 the Republic of Ireland and other OECD members agreed that the global minimum effective corporation tax rate will be 15% for any multinationals with revenues in excess of €750m.

In January 2017 the Northern Ireland power-sharing executive collapsed when Sinn Féin withdrew from it in a disagreement with the DUP about the financial administration of incentives intended to encourage the use of green energy. This was the so-called 'cash-for-ash' scandal. An official enquiry into the 'cash-for-ash' affair blamed inefficiency rather than corruption. There was also bad feeling between the two parties over the DUP's refusal to yield to Sinn Féin in respect to certain demands concerning the use of the old Irish or Gaelic language in Northern Ireland. The assembly now remained suspended until January 2020.

On 14 June 2017 a doctor of Indian descent became prime minister of the Republic, with Leo Varadkar replacing Enda Kenny as both leader of the right-of-centre Fine Gael party and *taoiseach*. In October 2022 Rishi Sunak, a businessman of Indian descent, became Prime Minister of the

United Kingdom of Great Britain and Northern Ireland. In 2023 Humza Yousaf, of Pakistani descent, became Scotland's first minister. It is a remarkable coincidence that all three are in power at the same time.

In 2017 too Zainab Boladale from Ennis, Co. Clare, became the first news anchor of Afro-Irish heritage on Irish national TV. Born in Nigeria, she has lived in Ireland from the age of four, learning the Irish language (Gaelic) and studying journalism at Dublin City University (DCU). In 2019 she was one of three people of Nigerian heritage who founded the Irish organisation 'Beyond Representation' in order to help people of colour who are breaking new ground in Irish media, arts and business to make connections. In 2020, Ireland's Economic and Research Institute found that most respondents openly supported more Black people coming to Ireland, but the majority dropped from 66% to 51% when respondents could conceal their attitudes. Salome Mbugua, a member of the Irish Human Rights and Equality Commission said 'The report comes at a moment when the relationship between individual attitudes and systemic racism has been cast into sharp focus.' Respondents were less likely to conceal negative attitudes when asked about Muslim immigrants.

The influx of people of many nationalities to live in Ireland, as in Britain, raises questions for this and future generations about what exactly it means to be 'Irish' or 'British'. On a more local level, people in Northern Ireland are asked the same question. They are in fact eligible to hold a UK and/or Irish passport. Ulster golfer Darren Clarke, once told *GolfDigest* (June 2008) 'I'm proud to be Irish, but I'm also Northern Irish. We have our own identity.' Clarke represented Ireland in international tournaments. Rory McIlroy, Ireland's top golfer in the second decade of the twenty-first century has found the question testing. Born to working class parents in Co. Down in 1989, Rory McIlroy was raised a Catholic and so might be assumed to consider himself simply 'Irish'. But he has indicated that he regards himself as both Irish and British. When it came to McIlroy's possible participation in the Olympic Games in Brazil in 2016 – which included golf for the first time since 1904 – would McIlroy decide to represent the UK or 'Ireland' (meaning in this context the team of the Republic of Ireland)? The British *Daily Mail* had quoted him saying 'I have grown up my whole life playing for Ireland under the Golfing Union of Ireland umbrella. But the fact is, I've always felt more British than Irish.' In the media and among the public on both sides of the Irish Sea the question gave rise to much speculation charged with political and nationalist undertones. McIlroy said that he might not participate at all, and might thus avoid offending anyone. He told the *Irish News* in Belfast 'I resent the Olympic Games because of the position it put me in, that's my feelings towards it, and whether that's right or wrong, it's how I feel' (*Irish News*, 13 Jan. 2017). Ultimately he agreed to play for Ireland at Rio, but then withdrew ostensibly because of a Zika virus scare in Brazil. He admitted that 'the whole politics of the thing' had also weighed on him. He did play for Ireland at the 2020 Olympics in Tokyo. McIlroy's fellow golfer and Northern Irishman Graeme McDowell, has told the BBC, 'We are in a very unique scenario in Northern Ireland. We could easily declare for Great Britain or we could easily declare for Ireland …. To me, golf is always an all-Ireland sport.'

A curious aspect of the Olympics is that the UK team is officially named 'Team GB' but represents Northern Ireland as well as Great Britain (England, Scotland and Wales). Given that British media commentators sometimes refer to Irish people who win prizes in sports as 'British' (to the amusement or annoyance of Irish nationalists), and that some Ulster unionists describe their own cultural identity as British, such 'brand' names have political and even imperialist implications. On the International Olympic Committee website the UK state appears simply as 'Great Britain'. When it comes to international football the United Kingdom is also unusual, because it is permitted to have four 'national' teams – one each from England, Wales, Scotland and Northern Ireland.

Early in 2018 Sinn Féin elected its first woman president, Mary Lou McDonald, a graduate of Trinity College Dublin and a *Dáil* deputy. This gave the party a 'soft' face compared to its image under 'hard men' such as Gerry Adams who had led it previously.

On 25 May 2018 a large majority of voters in the Republic supported the repeal of the 1983 constitutional amendment that had seen the electorate confirm the existing legal ban on abortion except where the mother's life was at risk. The eighth amendment was now replaced by a law permitting abortion without explanation in the first twelve weeks of pregnancy, and in defined health circumstances after that. The public had gradually been educated in the nuances of abortion policy during four referendum campaigns between 1983 and 2018. Abortions are now free of charge on the public health service in the Republic of Ireland, although the service nationally is uneven. The holding of referendums on key issues, as is required to change the Republic's written constitution, has had the beneficial effect of provoking informed debate and of thus ensuring that controversial proposals are well-aired and any changes clearly seen to have public support. Depending on judges to make controversial decisions that extend personal rights can lead to a public backlash, as arguably happened in the United States.

Meanwhile, liberal British abortion laws did not apply in Northern Ireland. Abortion proposals in the Northern Ireland Assembly were blocked by the Democratic Unionist Party, but from early 2020 abortions became legally possible there when the UK government authorised them despite the Northern Ireland Assembly's failure to do so. DUP leader Arlene Foster described the change as 'shameful'. Two years later the *Guardian* newspaper (4 May 2022) reported that abortion services were 'patchy to non-existent' in Northern Ireland.

In August 2018 Pope Francis visited Ireland for the 'World Meeting of Families'. While Irish people generally respect Francis, their reaction to his visit was underwhelming – with little excitement and crowds much smaller than those greeting Pope John Paul II in 1979. This reflected an altered relationship between Irish citizens and the Catholic Church. Yet through its ownership of educational and medical properties the Catholic Church retains some significant powers in teaching and health.

Also in 2018 the Irish government held a referendum to remove a constitutional requirement for a law of blasphemy, although there appears never to have been a prosecution for that offence in the Republic. The majority in favour was 2:1.

In June 2019 Donald Trump became the latest serving US president to visit Ireland, in his case largely to attend his exclusive golf course in Co. Clare (he has another in Scotland). He was welcomed locally by those who have benefited from his company's investment. There were protests against his climate and other policies. Trump informed people on arrival that he 'loves the Irish'. The BBC reported that during an impromptu press conference with *Taoiseach* Leo Varadkar, Trump said 'We have a border situation in the United States and you have one over here, but I hear it's going to work out very well.' Varadkar immediately made it clear that the Irish government wanted to avoid a new hard border 'or wall' between the Republic of Ireland and Northern Ireland.

The Northern Ireland Assembly was restored in January 2020, but almost immediately was overtaken by Brexit. The Democratic Unionist Party, along with some other unionists and some businesses objected strongly to new custom checks on goods crossing the Irish Sea. The checks that were set up as part of the Brexit Protocol agreement were needed because some goods coming to Ireland from Britain are destined for the Republic (and some destined onwards for other EU states). Unionist opponents regarded the sea checks as an internal United Kingdom border that weakened their connection to Britain.

In 2021 Arlene Foster resigned as first minister, partly blamed by unionist hardliners for the controversial Brexit Protocol relating to Northern Ireland and blamed too for the 'cash-for-ash' scandal that had seen public money misspent on a deeply flawed and inefficient renewable heating incentive scheme in Northern Ireland. She was succeeded by the DUP's Paul Givan, who himself resigned in February 2022, triggering once more the collapse of the Northern Ireland executive. The DUP, supported by right wing MPs of the British Conservative Party, threatened that unless there were changes to the protocol it would not participate again in a Northern Ireland executive, thus making power-sharing impossible under the terms agreed for it.

In early 2023 the UK government and the EU agreed on the 'Windsor Framework', which outlines changes in how the terms of the Northern Ireland Protocol are given effect. It was clear by then that many businesses and the farming sector in Northern Ireland saw advantages for themselves in the special EU Protocol arrangement already in place. But continuing objections by the DUP indicated just how difficult it is for the two main traditions in Ireland to work together when each has a fundamentally different vision of its political future.

The importance of Irish-American connections has been evident during this period. The United States Congress made it clear that there would be no major US trade deal with the UK outside the EU unless the Protocol dispute was settled. When Joe Biden was elected president in 2020, British and Irish TV stations showed a British correspondent calling out to him 'Mr. Biden, a quick word for the BBC,' and Biden – smiling as he walked away – replied 'The BBC? I'm Irish!' In 2023 Biden became the latest serving US president to visit Ireland. However, the Irish and Irish-Americans will not indefinitely retain their disproportionate influence in North American politics.

The Brexit dispute demonstrated to some voters in Northern Ireland the dangers of becoming captive to political extremes. If the DUP and Sinn Féin thought that people had settled into a pattern of inevitably voting for those two parties, the results of the UK general election of 2019 in Northern Ireland sent them a warning. It reflected dissatisfaction with the squabbling between the DUP and Sinn Féin that had seen the Northern Ireland Assembly suspended again. Both parties now won a reduced share of the vote for the province's eighteen seats at Westminster, with the DUP down 5.4% to 30.6% and the abstentionist Sinn Féin down 6.7% to 22.8%. The biggest gain at their expense was made by the centrist Alliance Party, winning 16.8% of the vote.

Meanwhile, in the Republic's general election of 8 February 2020, voters created a shockwave politically by returning an almost identical number of Fianna Fáil, Fine Gael and Sinn Féin deputies (35–38 each). Suddenly Sinn Féin, ostensibly a left-of-centre party but predominantly devoted to achieving an all-Ireland state, was also a major force in the Republic. There had emerged the real possibility that it could soon become even bigger and, as the largest party in parliament, form a government. For the first time the old rivals Fianna Fáil and Fine Gael combined to form a coalition administration, with support from the Green Party which had won a dozen seats. It was agreed that the leader of Fine Gael Leo Varadkar and the leader of Fianna Fáil Micheál Martin would take turns leading the government as *taoiseach*, for two and a half years each. The threat from Sinn Féin had driven together parties that grew out of the civil war of 1922–1923, a civil war over the terms of a settlement with Britain that created the independent Irish Free State (later the Republic of Ireland).

Also in February 2020 the first case of Covid-19 was confirmed in Ireland. On 9 March the Irish government cancelled all parades to mark the national holiday, St Patrick's Day (17 March). For the next two years there were lock-downs and vaccination programmes, as elsewhere.

On 1 January 2021 the Republic of Ireland, which is a militarily neutral state due partly to the Irish experience of British colonialism, became for one year an elected member of the United Nations Security Council. Membership of the United Nations itself has been central to the Irish state's foreign policy. Since joining the UN in 1955, Irish troops have served with the UN in the Congo, Cyprus, Lebanon and elsewhere. There is some debate in Ireland about Irish neutrality, but no substantial public support for joining NATO – notwithstanding the Russian invasion of Ukraine in 2022.

Into the Future

In March 2023 Holly Cairns TD became leader of the Social Democrats, one of the Republic's smallest political parties. In her mid thirties, she expressed a national mood among younger Irish people when she declared 'I am a member of the first ever generation who will be worse off than our parents. This did not happen by accident. Political choices made by successive Governments have resulted in the aspirations and dreams of an entire generation being either diminished or destroyed.' Support for her party immediately rose in the polls. There is a widespread feeling in the Republic that younger people today have been left unduly exposed to the hazards of the marketplace despite an ostensible economic recovery from the 2008 crash, a feeling expressed in the novels of Caoilinn Hughes for example. There is a particular problem regarding the ownership of apartments and houses. Prices are high and international vulture funds have been allowed to purchase entire developments at preferential unit prices. The number of publicly-funded homes being built is low, and the shortage of accommodation is exacerbated by a rise in the number of refugees – not least due to the war in Ukraine. At the same time, right-wing factions have tried to stir up anti-immigrant sentiment.

Yet it is also important to retain an historical perspective on today's problems. Ireland, including the new state that emerged in 1921–22, has survived worse vicissitudes. In 1841 the populations of England and what is now the Republic of Ireland were, approximately 14.8 million and 6.5 million respectively. Thus, only about twice as many people lived then in England as in the area that later became the Republic. During the 1840s the Great Famine devastated much of Ireland, with about one quarter of the population dying and another quarter emigrating. Afterwards, emigration continued to be a feature of Irish life. The population of the Republic of Ireland reached its lowest point in 1961, when it stood at 2.8 million, or less than half what it had been in 1841. About fifty-seven million people now live in England, but just over five million in the Republic. In other words, England has gone from having about twice the population of today's Republic of Ireland to having about eleven times more people.

Like people everywhere, the Irish must deal with objective realities that include climate change, global population growth, migration, automation and artificial intelligence. A key question is whether Irish people will do so eventually as one state, or as two separate political units.

Very recent opinion polls show clearly that being part of the Catholic/nationalist tradition does not mean that one is necessarily prepared at present to vote for Northern Ireland to join the Republic in an all-island state. Voters in the north ask if they would be better off in a united Ireland. How much longer will Britain subsidise Northern Ireland? People in the south ask what might unification cost the Republic, financially or otherwise? A vast majority agrees that unity should not be forced. The Irish constitution today includes this declaration:

> It is the firm will of the Irish nation, in harmony and friendship, to unite all the people who share the territory of the island of Ireland, in all the diversity of their identities and traditions, recognising that a united Ireland shall be brought about only by peaceful means with the consent of a majority of the people, democratically expressed, in both jurisdictions in the island.

Economic growth and social change in the Republic make it potentially more attractive than it used to be to people living in Northern Ireland. If the north once had a commercial edge over the independent state to the south, it has lost it. Economic as well as political co-operation can benefit the whole island, even in the absence of full unity.

A particular aspect of the Republic from which the Protestant majority in Northern Ireland long recoiled was the great influence of the Catholic hierarchy over public and private life. However, that influence has been largely shattered by both the process of modernisation and by a succession of scandals including clerical child abuse. Regular attendance at church has declined greatly and the hierarchy is highly unlikely to recover ever again a power that it long took for granted. Moreover, Irish life is now leavened by other cultures, with a significant proportion of the Republic's residents having been born outside Ireland. After Roman Catholics and members of the Protestant Church of Ireland, the third biggest faith group in the state now consists of Muslims.

A continuing divisive factor is that Northern Ireland, being part of the United Kingdom, is within the NATO military alliance. The Republic has long declared itself a neutral country and kept out of NATO. The proximity of Russian ships to the Irish coast in 2022 during the war in Ukraine, and applications by Finland and Sweden to join NATO, have raised questions about the wisdom of neutrality.

The Belfast/Good Friday Agreement of 1998, as endorsed by the public in referendums on each side of the Irish border, states that

> it is for the people of the island of Ireland alone, by agreement between the two parts respectively and without external

impediment, to exercise their right of self-determination on the basis of consent, freely and concurrently given, North and South, to bring about a united Ireland, if that is their wish, accepting that this right must be achieved and exercised with and subject to the agreement and consent of a majority of the people of Northern Ireland.

On 5 May 2022 Sinn Féin, which was already riding higher in opinion polls in the Republic than any other single party there, became the first nationalist party to be the largest of *all* parties in the Northern Ireland Assembly. It did so in what was the assembly's seventh election. The result gave the party the right to nominate its vice-president Michelle O'Neill as Northern Ireland's first minister. The remarkable political rise of Sinn Féin north and south of the border alarms unionists, amongst others on both sides of the Irish border, because of the party's long-term association with the IRA. If a bare majority of the electorate in Northern Ireland is somehow persuaded to support unity, but if a majority of Protestants or unionists there still opposes it, will Sinn Féin try to force a vote on the question? What then for all Ireland?

ADDITIONAL READING

Ben Collins, *Irish Unity: Time to Prepare* (Edinburgh, 2022)

Stephen Collins, *Ireland's Call: Navigating Brexit* (Dublin, 2022)

Colin Coulter, Niall Gilmartin, Katy Hayward and Peter Shirlow, *Northern Ireland A Generation after Good Friday: Lost Futures and New Horizons in the 'Long Peace'* (Manchester, 2021)

Diarmaid Ferriter, *The Transformation of Ireland 1900–2000* (London, 2004)

Mark Henry, *In Fact: An Optimist's Guide to Ireland at 100* (Dublin, 2021)

Colum Kenny, *Moments that Changed Us* (Dublin, 2005)

Mary Kenny, *The Way We Were: Catholic Ireland since 1922* (Dublin, 2022)

Mo Mowlam, *Momentum: The Struggle for Peace, Politics and the People* (London, 2002)

Deirdre Nuttall, *Different and the Same: A Folk History of the Protestants of Independent Ireland* (Dublin, 2020)

Fintan O'Toole, *We Don't Know Ourselves: A Personal History of Ireland since 1958* (London, 2021)